Sky full of
Dreams

Sky full of
DREAMS

the Aviation Exploits, Creations,
and Visions of
Bruce K. Hallock

Austin Bruce Hallock

Corvallis, Oregon
ElevonBooks.com

Copyright © 2010 by Bruce G. Hallock (writing as Austin Bruce Hallock).

All rights reserved. No part of this publication may be reproduced, stored in a retrieval system, or transmitted, in any form or by any means, electronic, mechanical, photocopying, recording, or otherwise, without the prior written permission of the publisher.

ISBN 978-0-9826390-0-9

Library of Congress Control Number: 2010921854

*In memory of my father
and for my mother*

Contents

Acknowledgements   ix

Prologue   1
    Events: Seeing his first airplane.
    Aircraft Described: Curtiss JN-4 Jenny.

1. Getting Airborne   5
    Events: Early aviation influences • model building • Cleveland Air Races • first airplane ride.
    Aircraft: Airship Akron • Waterman Arrowbile • Stinson Detroiter (monoplane).

2. Leaving the Nest   14
    Events: College • working at Wright Field.
    Aircraft: Hallock Bobtail (model) • Northrop N1M • B-17 • P-38 Lightning • SB2C Helldiver • XB-19 • Waco XCG-4A • Sikorsky XR-4 • Hallock Baffle Bird (model).

3. War and Romance   29
    Events: Joining the Navy • first solo • basic flight training • multi-engine training.
    Aircraft: Piper Cub • Timm N2T Tudor • Stearman Kaydet (N2S) • N3N • Junkers Ju-88 • SNV • SNB.

4. Flying Boats and Wedding Bells   44
    Events: Flying Navy transports • marriage • buying his first airplane.
    Aircraft: PBM • R4D • Aeronca Chief.

5. New Horizons at War's End   63
    Events: More adventures with the Aeronca and a tour of duty in the Philippines.
    Aircraft: Aeronca Chief • R4D • F6F Hellcat • PQ-14.

6. Airport Schemes and Grander Dreams   75
    Events: Air charter and flight-instruction business • Austin Aero Service • designing and building his first airplane.
    Aircraft: Aeronca Champion • Stinson 108 Voyager • Cessna Bobcat (UC-78) • Hallock HT-1 Road Wing (Road-A-Plane) • Fulton Airphibian • Taylor Aerocar • ConVairCar • Aeronca Sedan.

7. **Bush Pilot and Fish Monger**   98
   EVENTS: Flying lobster from British Honduras • more work on the Road Wing • crop dusting.
   AIRCRAFT: Noorduyn Norseman (UC-64) • Hallock HT-1 Road Wing (Road-A-Plane).

8. **Away with the Norseman**   111
   EVENTS: Flying down to Peru • working on the Cutlass at Chance Vought • a federal indictment and trial.
   AIRCRAFT: Noorduyn Norseman (UC-64) • F7U Cutlass.

9. **From Executive Pilot to Test Pilot**   125
   EVENTS: Working as an executive pilot • test flights and further development of the Road Wing • a trip down the Pan American Highway.
   AIRCRAFT: Beech 18 (Twin Beech) • Lockheed Lodestar • DC-3 • de Havilland Dove • Hallock HT-1 Road Wing.

10. **Politicians and Rickshaws**   142
    EVENTS: Flying for LBJ and other big shots • designing and building the Motor Rickshaw.
    AIRCRAFT: Beech 18 (Twin Beech) • Lockheed Lodestar • Convair 240 • de Havilland Dove.

11. **Building a Better Airplane**   158
    EVENTS: Designing and building the Aero Wing.
    AIRCRAFT: Hallock HT-2 Caravan • Hallock Aero Wing.

12. **Top Secrets and Emergency Landings**   177
    EVENTS: More executive piloting and consulting • working as pilot for the Applied Research Lab.
    AIRCRAFT: Beech 18 (Twin Beech) • TC-47K (DC-3).

13. **Pterodactyl and Friends**   194
    EVENTS: Buying and flying the Navion • EAA activities • designing and building the Pterodactyl • test piloting the Smith Mini-Plane • flying the Windecker Eagle
    AIRCRAFT: Ryan Navion B • Hallock Pterodactyl • Smith Mini-Plane • Windecker Eagle.

Epilogue   218

Index   221

About the Author   230

Acknowledgements

Although a book may have a single author's name on the cover, few if any published works owe their existence to only one person. This book is no exception. It did not even begin with me, but with my brother Don Hallock, who has for decades been diligently collecting bits of aviation history—especially items related to our father. In early 2004 he approached me with the idea for this book. His timing was most felicitous. At that time, no one imagined that in less than two years our father would be gone from this world. Don helped with much of the interviewing and research and of course contributed some remembrances of his own. He also provided many of the photographs and created most of the representational drawings and other artwork.

My mother Enid Hallock also took a keen interest in the project and helped immensely by conducting and writing down some of the preliminary interviews and providing open access to all her papers, including her private diaries. And of course her memories served as a primary source for much of the anecdotal information herein.

My wife Leela Devi deserves martyr status for putting up with me through this time-consuming project and for serving as first reader on the drafts of each chapter.

I owe special thanks to a host of other relatives and friends who contributed in various ways, large and small. I list most of them here in no particular order.

Macy M. Hallock, brother of Bruce K. Hallock, offered certain details that helped me flesh out the segments set in Medina, Ohio, and Miami, Florida. John Dana supplied invaluable information on the subject of antique model-airplane engines. Charles Quist, Matt Roberts, and Jim Newman were all very gracious and generous in relating their memories of St. Edwards Airport and other relevant events. Connie and Koert Voorhees both provided several useful remembrances. The crop-dusting episode would have been sparse indeed without Malcolm Lauderdale's colorful reminiscences. Peter Coltman helped me accurately portray the drama of landing a heavily loaded Twin Beech on a short runway in a high crosswind. Ted Cloer was kind enough to sit with me for an afternoon and relate a wealth of information and vivid stories on the subject of the Applied Research Laboratories and his flying adventures with my father. John Langston provided invaluable insight into the construction of the Pterodactyl. Dr. Ron Stearman eagerly and thoroughly responded to my list of questions concerning the Windecker Eagle and his experiences with my father. Jay Miller supplied some poignant recollections as well as advice and guidance on the draft manuscript. My brother Gary Hallock also offered useful comments on portions of the manuscript.

I am also grateful for the diligent assistance provided by the staff of the Flint Public Library and the Lyndon B. Johnson Presidential Library.

And I owe an immense debt of gratitude to my good friend Michael Ambrose for his diligent proofing, copyediting, and advice in helping me move this book beyond the manuscript stage.

— Austin Bruce Hallock

Prologue

A fine fall day in the mid 1920s. The Medina, Ohio, County Fair. A crowd gathers around a Curtiss Jenny parked at one end of the racetrack. The airplane is a major attraction this year.

From the crowd five-year-old Bruce K. Hallock peers at the strange machine. Like many others on this day, he is getting his first glimpse of a real airplane. His father has brought him to see the flying machine.

Across the country, similar scenes are playing out. Less than a decade earlier, the end of the Great War had stranded hundreds of these two-seater biplanes — brand new, crated up, poised for overseas shipment. When the government began disposing of the surplus trainers, enterprising individuals could pick them up for as little as $50. And so began the age of barnstorming, which introduced the airplane to many small-town Americans during the Roaring Twenties.

Young Bruce's innate curiosity about mechanical things compels him to work his way up close to the plane. He touches the wings. He runs his hand over the taught linen fabric. He inspects the wheels. And that's when something doesn't seem right.

Bruce has learned that other motor vehicles — automobiles, tractors, etc. — have some sort of connection between the engine and the wheels. But the airplane seems to have nothing to make the wheels go around. So he asks his dad about this.

Macy Orsen Hallock's easy familiarity with machines and tools, his worldly knowledge, and his fatherly indulgence give him immense credibility with the boy. And he has seen airplanes before in New York where he had grown up. So his authoritative explanation of the concept of the propeller seems plausible enough. He refers to it as "an airscrew." His finger makes a spiraling motion. "It's like a drill going through wood," he says. "It pulls the plane through the air. The wheels don't need to be powered."

Bruce accepts this answer — provisionally. "But do the wheels turn when it flies?" he asks.

His father assured him that they do not. The airplane's wheels do not make the plane go — therefore they don't turn during flight.

Satisfied, young Bruce directs his curiosity to other matters. There was much to wonder about.

After centuries of dreaming, human beings have finally taken wing. And two decades after the first manned, powered flight, a new generation is transfixed. The flying machine has begun to prove itself. A new realm has opened up. The excitement is palpable. The air buzzes with possibilities. Imaginations soar — especially those of young boys. Bruce is the perfect age, and no one feels the thrill more than he.

When it's time for the plane to fly, Bruce and his father make their way to the grandstand. At the other end of the racetrack, trees have been cut down to give the airplane more clearance. There is some trouble starting the engine, which heightens the suspense. Finally the eight-cylinder OX-5 clatters to life, and the airplane trundles into position at the end of the field. Bruce's critical eye takes in details — the shape of the tail, the proportions of wing and fuselage.

Suddenly the Jenny makes an ungainly rush down the field. Its speed mounts. The tail lifts, and the ship bounces into the air to a chorus of astonished *ahs!* It flies right by the grandstand. Bruce can't help noticing the spoked wheels. They are spinning. The airplane is flying through the air, and its wheels are going around and around!

The confused boy glances up at his dad, who seems totally unaware that his credibility had just taken a nosedive.

* * *

The stories in this book are all true. However, readers should bear in mind that they are tales handed down from a father to his still-impressionable sons. Where possible the author has verified facts, but many details stand solely on the word of Bruce King Hallock himself, a man whose imagination remained to the end immersed in the intoxicating adventure of flight.

Chapter 1
GETTING AIRBORNE

What sets the course of a life—especially one so focused on a single field of endeavor? Maybe the Jenny at the fair was the seminal event. Or perhaps the course had been set earlier by ineluctable forces, the tenor of the times. Or possibly a series of later events propelled young Bruce King Hallock on his life's path. Whatever the answer, aviation and dreams of flight came to dominate his thoughts at an early age. After seeing the Jenny, Bruce started building models "like crazy"—his own words. But he was still very young, so these weren't flying models. He compulsively assembled odd pieces of wood into airplane shapes. He gleaned every clue a young boy could about the nature of these wonderful machines.

Meanwhile aviation began making big news. Charles Lindbergh's 1927 solo flight across the Atlantic Ocean amazed the world and expanded aviation's prospects. Designers were thinking big.

Toward the end of the decade, over in Akron, Ohio, just 18 miles from Medina, the Goodyear-Zeppelin Co. began construction on a gigantic rigid-hull dirigible. More than once, Bruce's father took him and his younger brother to see the big duralumin skeleton under construction inside the largest free-standing building in the world. When finished, the *Akron*, named for the city of her birth, would measure 785 feet from stem to stern. At a cost of $4.5 million, it would be the most expensive aircraft ever built. Eight 12-cylinder engines mounted inside the hull would drive propellers through shafts. It would be a true ship of the air.

By 1931 the U.S. Navy had the *Akron* in service. And everywhere it went, it made news.

Bruce K. Hallock, five years old.

Spirit of the times — 1920s-era model airplane kit advertisement.

USS Akron airship under construction and in flight.

* * *

"Extra! Extra! Read all about it! Airship *Akron* to fly over Medina tonight!"

Newsboys brandishing full-spread, illustrated stories passed in front of Hallock's Music Store on West Liberty Street. Macy Orsen Hallock had owned and operated the store since 1916, the same year he'd married Clara Ulmer. They had met in the local bank where she had worked as a teller. Now they had four children and made their home in the apartment above the store. Clara Louise was the oldest. Bruce, born April 28, 1921, was second. Then came brother Macy Monroe and baby Helen.

The music store was a family business. Mrs. Hallock demonstrated new sheet music on the piano for customers. The store sold instruments, Victrolas, and 78 rpm records. They also carried a variety of other merchandise and appliances, such as Tapen stoves and Singer sewing machines. On Saturday evenings when the farmers came to town to buy supplies, a small ensemble sometimes performed in front of the store. And in the basement, Uncle Walter ran a bar, a place where Bruce's strict Methodist mother forbade him to venture.

But on this evening, all thoughts had turned skyward. Everyone wanted to see the great airship fly over. And with access to the flat roof above their apartment, the Hallocks had the perfect viewing gallery. So they made a party of it, invited friends, and had dinner on the roof. Others gathered on nearby rooftops. Laughter and music drifted on the clear evening air while eager eyes scanned the western sky.

Perhaps the event might be compared to a present-day overflight of a space shuttle. But in an era of fewer diversions and meager mass communication (even radios and phones weren't common), the impending visitation generated a more palpable public excitement.

At last a dot of light came into view accompanied by a distant, low hum. The music stopped. The droning grew louder. People pointed and exclaimed with excitement as the colossal cigar shape appeared out of the night. Lit from within and without, the silver *Akron* sailed over downtown Medina, propelled by the robust thrum of eight 560-hp Maybach engines. The newspapers had supplied all the basic data: 6,500,000 cubic feet of helium, a crew of 80, cruising speed 55 knots. And in her belly, four Curtiss Sparrowhawk scouts awaited deployment. Like bees protecting a hive, the little biplanes could drop from an opening, perform missions, and return to the mother ship via a mechanized trapeze extended below the hangar compartment. But on this night, the impressive facts and figures paled beside the sheer wonder of this Jules Verne vision overhead.

And then it was gone.

By 1933 the *Akron* would be wrecked in a storm, and two years later, her sister ship, the *Macon*, would also meet disaster. The glory days of the big airships were already drawing to a close.

* * *

Meanwhile Bruce's dreams were soaring. He wanted to make things fly, so he got serious about model building. In the early 1930s Quaker Oats offered a flying model airplane kit in exchange for two box tops and ten cents. Twelve-year-old Bruce mailed in the required remittance and received a package containing balsa wood blanks, longerons, rubber band, tissue paper, a tube of glue, and a page of instruction diagrams. With some help from his dad, he built the plane — a low-wing Curtiss pursuit. It flew — but not very well.

However lackluster that first plane's performance, it did not discourage further efforts. Bruce issued himself a personal challenge to build better planes. He started reading everything he could find at the library, particularly *Popular Aviation* (which later became *Flying* magazine). And more models followed — many more. The mailman carried off a succession of envelopes containing box tops with coins attached. These box-top models were mostly planes of World War I and the National Air Races. Bruce also found some good model kits in stores for 15 to 25 cents. But before long he was designing his own.

Bruce's enthusiasm for model building drew in friends. He and his buddies formed a club, the Medina Model Makers. And they all joined the American Modelers Association (which later became the Academy of Model Aeronautics); the membership fee was $1. Bruce was club president.

The boys liked to visit nearby Bowman's Flying Field, where barnstormers sometimes showed up on Sundays. Every flight was an event, followed by a passing of the hat to help pay expenses. A hawker with a megaphone would try to entice daring spectators to take a ride. In the background little stick-and-tissue marvels soared briefly, vying for a share of the attention.

The Hallocks, 1934. Left to right: Clara Ulmer (mother), Macy Monroe, Helen, Bruce, Clara Louise, and Macy Orsen (father).

The Medina Model Makers Club, March 1939. Pictured left to right (according to the newspaper), kneeling: Bruce K. Hallock, Robert Effinger, and Duane Todd. Standing: Macy Monroe Hallock, Jack Bennett, Ronald Partlon, Floyd McKain, Floyd Ganyard, Wade Gensemer, and Fred Koehler.

Bruce and his friend Bob Effinger were the club's two most prolific model builders. Sometimes they hitchhiked over to Akron. A used bookstore there would take two old magazines in trade for one. Secondhand periodicals could also be purchased for a nickel apiece. The boys loaded up on *Model Airplane News*, *Popular Aviation*, *Air Trails*, and any other relevant publications. They scoured the pages for information they could use to improve their designs.

The father of one of the club members, Floyd Bennett, Sr., was a graduate of Case Institute of Technology in Cleveland. He arranged for the model airplane club to visit the wind tunnel at the college. Dr. John R. Weske (who would later play a significant role in Bruce's career) showed how the wind tunnel was used to determine the lift and stability features of a given design. Bruce proudly lent one of his own models for the demonstration.

Model airplanes of the day were predominantly rubber powered with hand-carved, wooden propellers. Of course every boy yearned for one of the new gasoline model engines, but at ten Depression-era dollars apiece, owning one seemed an impossible dream. And there matters might have stood, if not for a Worthington Wholesale Hardware catalog that arrived at the music store. As a retail merchant, Mr. Hallock could obtain the Brown Junior engines at a discount. And Bruce discovered that purchasing a half-dozen lot would bring the cost down to $6.75 apiece—still a substantial sum, but not inconceivable.

With some effort the club members raised the funds, and Mr. Hallock picked up the engines on his next trip to Cleveland. Bruce's gasoline-powered model—an original design—was the first to fly.

* * *

Aviation firsts were also being achieved in the wider world. New speed, altitude, and endurance records kept the public fascinated. Many of these advances were showcased at the annual National Air Races in Cleveland. The races had first been brought to Cleveland's Hopkins Field in 1929 by a consortium of civic groups and local

One of Bruce's early gas models.

businesses. The big Labor Day weekend event proved so successful at this venue that it continued in Cleveland (with only a couple of exceptions) through 1939 and then for a while again after World War II until it was curtailed. During its heyday, the event drew crowds numbering in the hundreds of thousands. Newspapers worldwide reported the race results and fully covered other associated flying events.

Two types of races were involved. In addition to the closed-course pylon races, which included the Thompson and Greve events, cross-country races starting in other parts of the nation (such as the Bendix race) were timed to reach Cleveland during the Labor Day weekend.

Bruce, along with his father and younger brother Macy, attended most of the races during the 1930s. He witnessed all of Roscoe Turner's wins, including his first Thompson victory in 1934. He saw the famous Granville Brothers' Gee Bee racers and Ben Howard's Damn Good Airplane (DGA) when it took both the Bendix and Thompson trophies in 1935. And he was there in 1937 to see Rudy Kling buzz past Earl Ortman's black Bromberg Special to win by the narrowest of margins.

But the long weekend event was more than races. Today we would call it an air show. The program included dead-stick landing contests, glider and autogiro demonstrations, blimp flights, parachute jumps, and performances by military aircraft. The latest ideas and innovations were on display, and some of these side exhibitions actually held the greatest allure for the budding aeronautical engineer.

In 1937 Waldo Waterman arrived at the races with his Arrowbile, a swept-wing, tailless pusher design. The airplane's wings were removable, and the stubby body, powered by its Studebaker auto engine, could be driven on the road. Waterman had even arranged to sell the planes at Studebaker dealerships.

Bruce recalled the impression the tailless design made on him. When he saw the Arrowbile fly, he thought: *Hey, that's neat! That's what I want to do — build a tailless airplane.*

So he carved out a couple of solid models to experiment with the concept. Unable to find much technical information on the subject, he experimented. Through trial and error, he achieved success with some tailless gliders and then gas-powered models. Something about the unconventional swept-wing form appealed to him, and it

Waterman Arrowbile.

would continue to hold his attention for decades to come.

* * *

Consumed as he was by aviation, certain other matters impinged on Bruce's life—matters such as high school and girls. The girls he claimed to have kept at arm's length. Biology was, for the time being, manageable. But biology the academic subject presented a greater challenge. As he struggled with the course work, his parents offered an incentive. "Make an *A* in biology," his dad said, "and you'll get an airplane ride."

Somehow Bruce made the grade. The payoff came later that year at a national model-plane convention held at the Akron municipal airport. His father handed over $2, and Bruce climbed into the backseat of a four-place Stinson Detroiter monoplane. What was his chief impression of that first airborne experience? In his own words: "I was disappointed in the lack of perception of great speed."

Stinson Detroiter monoplane.

Chapter 2
LEAVING THE NEST

Things were changing for the Hallock family. By the mid 1930s, they had moved into a new house on Akron Road, which at the time was five miles outside of town. Bruce often gazed wistfully at that straight stretch of road in front of the house, imagining an airplane using it for an impromptu landing strip, himself at the controls.

The family's business had changed too. What had begun as a side interest pursued by Mrs. Hallock in a backroom of the music store had burgeoned into a substantial antique business. Both Mr. and Mrs. Hallock found the new venture engaging and profitable enough to warrant opening up a full-fledged antique store on North Court Street. Eventually they sold the music store and focused their efforts on the new enterprise.

Bruce recalled having trouble answering questions about his father's occupation. In addition to being a retail merchant, M. O. Hallock dealt in real estate. And before marrying, he and his brother Tom had engineered and built fire engines on Ford Model T chassis. Bruce's own inclinations seemed to stem from this mechanical vein.

As high school graduation approached, Bruce's father and Floyd Bennett, Sr., both encouraged him to attend Case Institute of Technology (later to become Case Western Reserve University) in Cleveland. The experience with the wind tunnel probably helped decide the matter. Annual tuition, including room and board, came to $900.

* * *

With the question of college settled, Bruce turned to his big summer project—a little airplane of his own design called the Bobtail.

The Hallock Chemical Truck, fire engine built and marketed by Macy Orsen Hallock and brother Tom.

The 46-inch-wingspan flying model represented the culmination of his tailless design efforts up to that point. The general configuration resembled Waterman's Arrowbile: swept-wing pusher with vertical fins near the wingtips. But the Bobtail's styling set it apart. The sleek lines of its fuselage complemented the wings' brisk and curvaceous grace. Where the Arrowbile was squat and stout looking, the Bobtail appeared lean and nimble. The plane stood on a lanky tricycle landing gear as if poised to spring into the future. All in all, the blue-and-yellow Bobtail was a pleasure to look at.

And it flew well.

So toward summer's end, Bruce entered the Bobtail in the annual Scripps-Howard Junior National Air Races held at the Akron municipal airport. Modelers arrived from all parts of the country to compete in the various events. Most of the competitions focused on endurance, testing how long different types of models could stay aloft. The Bobtail's category was Original Design, which not only required that the plane perform but also show a certain innovative flair and distinctiveness as determined by the judges.

The air was calm, and it was a good day for flying. Hand-launched gliders corkscrewed up and floated on warm currents.

Tissue-covered, rubber-powered planes climbed toward the scanty clouds behind big paddle-like propellers. Over in the old blimp hangar, delicate film-covered wraiths described lazy circles in the stillness of the cavernous expanse. And all across the open field, gas engines shrieked as fliers tried for new records.

When it came time for his event, Bruce readied his plane. With one eye on his competitors' efforts, he fueled up and made a final check. Soon enough his turn came. He hooked up the booster battery, set the timing to full retard, and flipped the hand-carved three-blade prop. The little Atwood Phantom .276 engine yowled to life. Bruce adjusted the timing and disconnected the booster.

The crowd pulled back. The striking little tailless had generated considerable interest. A newsreel cameraman had set up nearby. Bruce set the Bobtail on the takeoff ramp, triggered the timer, and let her go. She scooted along the ramp and took to the air. Some bystanders uttered muffled exclamations, perhaps astonished at the unconventional design's viability. Others cheered encouragement.

The Bobtail climbed in a lazy left-hand spiral above the spectators and contestants. When the timer cut the engine, the plane transitioned smoothly into a glide, circling down in the opposite direction. Then as if guided by her designer's fondest hopes, the

Bruce's 1939 Bobtail.

free-flying Bobtail touched down on the concrete strip and rolled to a stop — right in front of the judges.

Years later when asked how he had managed that landing, Bruce only answered: "Danged if I know! It was the best flight it ever did."

Al Williams — record-setting aviator, chief Navy test pilot, and famous aerobatic performer — presented the first-prize "Louis W. Greve" trophy and a check for $25. Bruce grinned as cameras clicked and flashed.

A Scripps-Howard newspaper reporter urged Bruce to draw up the plans for the prize-winning Bobtail. The story and plans appeared in the *Cleveland Press*. Because of this publication, the Society of Antique Modelers today recognizes the Bobtail as an "eligible design" for its Old-Timer competitions.

The $25 bought an ivory slide rule with leather case.

* * *

In the fall of 1939, the champion aeromodeler and his new slide rule moved into the Beta Theta Pi fraternity house in Cleveland.

Bruce K. Hallock with his Bobtail and trophy, Akron, Ohio, 1939.

Bruce wanted to become an aeronautical engineer, but Case Institute of Technology did not offer that degree. So he majored in mechanical engineering and took Dr. John R. Weske's courses in aeronautics. He also landed a part-time job in the school's aeronautics lab.

Being out in the world among like-minded enthusiasts was a heady experience. And Dr. Weske went out of his way to kindle his students' interests. Weske was an avid pilot and personal friend of C. Gilbert Taylor, founder of the Taylorcraft Corporation. Bruce toured the Taylorcraft factory in Alliance, Ohio, with Dr. Weske and a group of other students eager to see the sturdy two-seaters under construction.

Bruce's model-building activities continued and even intensified. He joined a Cleveland club called the Balsa Butchers, where he made the acquaintance of Dick Korda and Chester Lanzo, already well-known figures in the world of flying models and destined to become legends. Bruce's skill at carving propellers earned friends. To save time on his journeys about town, he adopted the habit of carving while riding the streetcar. Most of the props he used himself. "I went through them pretty fast," he recalled.

On weekends, the Balsa Butchers rode the streetcar with their airplanes to the end of the line and then walked about a mile to a favorite flying field. It was at this field on the outskirts of Cleveland that Bruce met Al Smithfield, who became a fast friend. Besides his keen interest in model airplanes, Al had a car and a wife who liked to cook. So Bruce enjoyed many a dinner of fried chicken, corn on the cob, and mashed potatoes and gravy at their home.

By this time all of Bruce's models were original designs. He made it a point of pride never to build airplanes from kits. And most of his designs were tailless. Waterman's Arrowbile and the success of the Bobtail had focused his interest. The more Bruce considered the novel concept, the more intrigued he became. He talked with Dr. Weske about tailless airplanes. The professor was encouraging, but this was not his specific area of interest. So Bruce gleaned what information he could from the libraries at Case and from other sources.

The Burgess-Dunne tailless designs of World War I had pioneered the concept, taking it beyond the experimental stage. Since then Germany's Alexander Lippisch had been developing his Storchs and delta designs. And in the U.S., Jack Northrop was also making progress with flying wings.

Tailless designs seemed to embody the most advanced thinking of the time. And Bruce discerned a certain economy and beauty inherent in the unorthodox planform. A wing that provided both lift and stabilization struck him as intrinsically elegant, a more refined blend of form and function. French designer Charles Fauvel may have made the case most forthrightly when he said of the standard aircraft layout: "The biggest part of the fuselage exists for nothing more than a link to the tail and adds nothing but weight for no other apparent contribution."

The time seemed right for a new approach, and Bruce was at the age when uninhibited enthusiasm can combine with growing knowledge to spark fresh ideas. So more wood shavings fell on the streetcar floorboards, and more swept-wing wonders soared over the field at the edge of town.

Meanwhile clouds of war swelled around the world. In Europe, the conflict that would become World War II had broken out. Japan was on the march across Asia. The U.S. remained, for the time, precariously neutral.

And at Case Institute of Technology, the academic year ground on. Bruce struggled with English and History but excelled at mechanical drawing, a skill that would stand him in good stead for years to come.

During the summer of 1940, Bruce persuaded his father to shell out $400 so he could attend a surveying camp sponsored by the college. For three weeks, he tromped around the Ohio countryside with transits, rods, and chains. He slept in a tent. When it was over, he had a new set of skills and a deep sunburn.

* * *

In September Bruce registered for the newly instituted military draft and returned to Case. Certain subjects remained problematic, while he excelled at others. He continued working part-time with the wind tunnel and helping Dr. Weske in the aeronautics lab. And of course he still flew models with the Balsa Butchers on the weekends. But more and more, his dreams assumed a grander scale. He began sketching designs for real planes.

By the end of the spring semester, Bruce had decided to suspend his academic studies and join the workforce. Embarking on his job search, his thoughts turned at once to Cleveland Pneumatic Tool Company, which had been one of the sponsors of the 1939 model airplane contest in Akron. After winning the prize for original design, Bruce had (at his father's urging) written a letter of thanks to Louis William "Papa" Greve, an executive officer of the company and also one of the principal backers of the Cleveland Air Races. Greve had written back, inviting Bruce to drop by sometime. Through this connection, he soon found employment as a draftsman for Cleveland Pneumatic Tool, the company that had developed the Cleco fastener used to temporarily hold sheet metal in place until rivets are put in. Bruce worked with the team designing the hydraulic landing gear for the B-25. He put drawings together on long pieces of paper and took change orders from the drawing department to the engineering department on the factory floor. This allowed him to see the process from inception to manufacture, an experience he regarded as invaluable.

During this time, Bruce lived in a Cleveland boarding house. The rent was $7 a week, which included one meal—Sunday dinner.

His stint with Cleveland Pneumatic Tool lasted only a couple of months. He would have stayed longer, but in August of 1941 another opportunity opened up that he could not resist. Dewey

Eldred, a friend of Dr. Weske's, had a seaplane operation at the Ninth Street Pier in downtown Cleveland as well as a more permanent flying business at Lost Nation Airport in nearby Willoughby, Ohio, on Lake Erie. Eldred was an innovative aviation pioneer who held several light-plane speed and endurance records. He had established one of his cross-country records in a Taylorcraft fitted with gasoline-filled floats. Eldred needed a draftsman to work on the drawings for a new airplane he was designing. Weske recommended Bruce, who took the job at $25 per week. Bruce actually worked in a small space in Dr. Weske's office, drawing mostly pontoons. While working for Eldred, Bruce had a couple of informal flying lessons at the seaplane base — one in a Piper Cub and another in a Stinson 105.

All seemed well, but within two months this dream job petered out. Eldred couldn't afford to keep his young draftsman on (though he did eventually build the airplane). So Bruce found work on the night shift at Cleveland Graphite Bronze foundry, a manufacturer of bushings and bearings. The pay was 65 cents per hour. It was hard manual labor, and he was unable to sleep during the day. After three sleepless weeks, he quit, determined to find a better way to stay solvent.

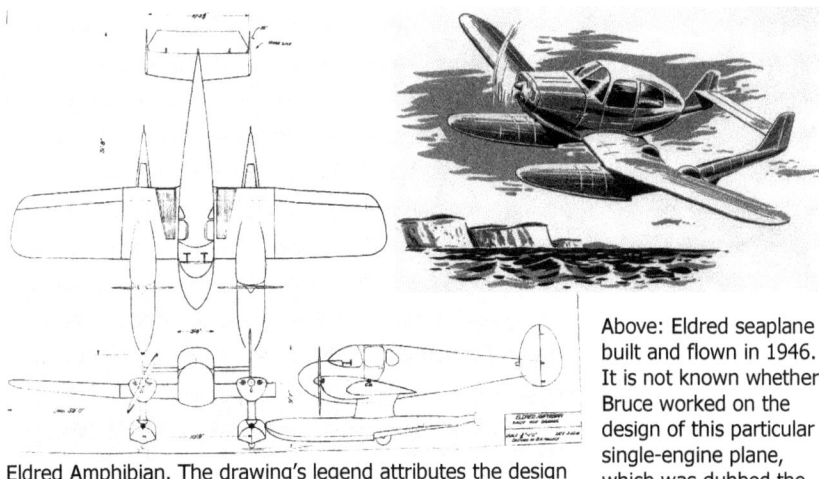

Eldred Amphibian. The drawing's legend attributes the design of this twin-engine to Bruce K. Hallock, 1941. Airplane was probably never built.

Above: Eldred seaplane built and flown in 1946. It is not known whether Bruce worked on the design of this particular single-engine plane, which was dubbed the "Flyer's Dream."

Again Dr. Weske helped out. The professor wrote to his friend Dr. Frank Wattendorf at Wright Field in Dayton, Ohio. Wright Field was home to a major facility for military aviation research and development. Wattendorf, who was civilian director of wind tunnels for the new Army Air Force, had helped design the 40,000-hp wind-tunnel complex at Wright Field. Weske gave Bruce a glowing recommendation, and an interview was arranged. Bruce traveled to Dayton, but through some mix-up, Dr. Wattendorf was out of town. Disappointed, Bruce returned to Cleveland only to find a telegram requesting that he report for work in Dayton the following Monday.

* * *

In early November 1941, Bruce's father helped him move across the state to Dayton and find a room. This son of Medina had never been so far from home, and his father left him with a reassuring hug.

On Monday morning Bruce went to work in the Weight and Balance Lab under Stan Hall. He checked weight and balance of

Wright Field, December 1941.

experimental planes and others newly arrived from the manufacturer. This involved verifying paperwork rather than checking the actual planes. He never found any gross errors in the measurements.

The job allowed him to see all the experimental and new airplanes passing through the facility. Years later, his wife would note that, upon seeing a new plane entering service, Bruce often commented: "I saw that years ago at Wright Field."

One of the many exciting events Bruce witnessed was the arrival for military tests of the Northrop N1M, a twin-engine flying wing. This small airplane, built of wood, was one of a series of flying proof-of-concept designs that eventually led to the much larger postwar XB-35 and jet-powered YB-49 flying wings.

Seeing the Northrop and other such experimental designs further stimulated Bruce's enthusiasm for the tailless configuration. At some point he hit upon the idea of authoring a comprehensive book on tailless airplanes. He wanted to chronicle their historical development and explore in depth all the aerodynamic and structural issues associated with the planform. To this end he spent many odd hours reading and writing at Wright Field's extensive aviation library.

Exposure to all this aeronautical innovation had another effect. It encouraged Bruce's visionary tendencies while also providing valuable schooling in the technicalities of the design and testing process. This interplay between what he saw and learned at work and his own evolving ideas generated a frothy synergy. So perhaps it was inevitable that he would also initiate his own parallel design program. Surrounded as he was by military aviation, he sketched his own visions of tailless fighters and bombers. But his true interests ran toward civilian aircraft, and he soon embarked on a project that embodied his ultimate ambition. Not yet ready or able to build a full-scale airplane, he conceived a large, realistic flying model of a four-seater — another swept-wing, tailless pusher.

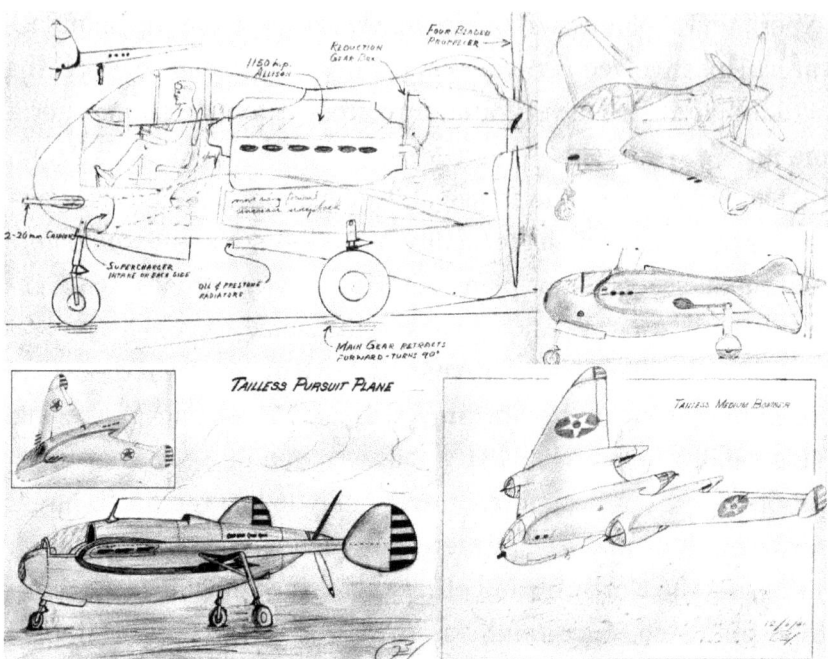
Some of Bruce's early military tailless reveries.

Bruce began work on his big tailless model soon after arriving in Dayton. By December, he had moved into a second-floor room at Mrs. Shawn's home. One fine Sunday morning found him in that room, at his drawing table, working on the plans. Nearby his radio played softly.

Everyone living then would remember that day of infamy — where they were and what they were doing when the newscaster broke in. "We interrupt this program..." All over the country activity froze. Conversations ceased, and attention focused on radio consoles. "The Japanese Imperial Forces have attacked Pearl Harbor in Hawaii."

Agitated, Bruce ran downstairs. "We're at war!" he told Mrs. Shawn, "We're going to war!" Instinctively the shaken twenty-year-old realized that the event would change his life.

The Pearl Harbor attack came only a month after Bruce had started at Wright Field, but anyone who had been there for even a single day before December 7, 1941, would have noticed the changed mood. With the nation now at war, the activities at this advanced research and testing facility in the heart of America suddenly took on new urgency. Because of Wright Field's importance to the war effort, Bruce would continue there under a deferment for almost another year before putting on a uniform.

* * *

President Roosevelt called for the production of 60,000 aircraft by the end of 1942 and another 100,000 by the end of 1943. But the procurement of military aircraft was (and still is) a complicated process involving close cooperation with the private sector. Generals and other high-level officials decided on future strategic equipment needs, such as night bombers, fighter planes, and torpedo bombers. Specifications were drafted and distributed to the private sector as requests for proposals. Interested companies submitted their proposals for specific designs, so-called paper airplanes. From these proposals the government selected two or three to be built on an experimental basis, designating each with an X— such as the XP-38 (the *P* in this case standing for *pursuit*). After a company built such an experimental plane and put it through a series of preliminary tests, it often went to Wright Field for further testing by the government.

Bruce witnessed this testing process up close and personal. He spent a great deal of time in the wind tunnel and in other testing areas. He hung around before and after work, during lunch, and on weekends. He watched the static stress testing, which involved bags of buckshot. A B-17 was turned upside down and the bags were placed on its wings to test for positive Gs, then right-side up for negative Gs.

Bruce had security clearance for all areas of the facility, *except* the place he most wanted to go—the experimental design lab where the really fanciful thinking was going on. But he still managed to see plenty. His first sight of a P-38 with engines running at full power induced tears of excitement. Later he actually got to hop aboard and ride in the buddy seat of this soon-to-be famous fighter.

Bruce took full advantage of a practice that allowed engineers to sign up for rides in the experimental planes. Many of these test flights were aboard cargo planes and bombers undergoing weight and balance checks, which involved repositioning loads (typically bags of buckshot) while airborne. Bruce served as shot-bag shifter on a test flight of a Curtiss SB2C Helldiver, a dive bomber that would later become notorious for its poor low-speed stability and dangerous stalling characteristics.

Other flight opportunities were even more extraordinary. Bruce went up in the Sikorsky XR-4, which later evolved into the military's first production helicopter. He got to ride in the XB-19, the largest bomber built until the postwar B-36. He flew aboard glider tow planes and in the gliders themselves. He rode in a British Airspeed Horsa, the big all-wood combat invasion glider, which was undergoing tests at Wright Field. And he was aboard a Waco XCG-4A glider the first time it ever carried a Jeep aloft. "When we got up there," he said, "we celebrated by starting the Jeep's engine and tooting the horn." The test records probably omitted any mention of a honking glider descending on Wright Field.

From the several *X*-designated aircraft submitted to meet a certain requirement, the military would select one for further evaluation and testing, and order a run of ten or so. These would be designated with a *Y*—such as the YP-38. Then after some inevitable modifications and changes, if all went well, the design would move into mass production, dropping the *Y* designation, as did the P-38. Of course most *X* and *Y* designs never progressed beyond the testing and evaluation stage, and Bruce considered himself lucky to get a good look at several of these might-have-beens.

Not all military aircraft were developed and approved through this paper-airplane-*X*-*Y* route. Manufacturers could build airplanes on speculation or offer existing types for evaluation. Many designs originally intended for civilian use entered military service in this manner, including the Douglas DC-3 and the Lockheed Lodestar, which became the C-47 and C-56 respectively, both yeoman workhorses of World War II. A man Bruce had known at Cleveland Pneumatic Tool had developed a small twin-engine airplane, which he wanted to sell to the military. He brought the plane to Wright Field and asked Bruce to help him get it considered. Bruce didn't really have that kind of influence, which was just as well, as he wasn't very impressed with the plane anyway.

* * *

Meanwhile in a realm where Bruce did have some influence, his own dream airplane was taking form. His landlady Mrs. Shawn had allowed him to set up a workshop in her basement. There the giant tailless model airplane reached completion. Its cabin doors opened on a detailed one-quarter-scale interior. The wings spanned over eight feet. Few model-flying sites could accommodate the behemoth, so it was flown on a tether fixed to a center post. The big model—affectionately called the *Baffle Bird*—represented a bridge

Baffle Bird flying model fuselage. Note realistic detail.

between Bruce's fanciful boyhood designs and his more mature visions. It delineated his future full-scale efforts, revealing the shape of things to come—after the war.

Bruce with his nearly finished Baffle Bird model. Wingspan exceeded eight feet.

Chapter 3
WAR AND ROMANCE

Bruce knew his time as a civilian was running out, and he was determined to enlist before his deferment expired and the draft caught up with him. Young and innocent as he may have been, he knew enough to dread the infantry. And anyway, he believed his talents lay elsewhere. He wanted to aid the war effort in a way that would best serve his country and himself. So aviation seemed like a natural fit — and an agreeable alternative to grunthood.

And the stars did seem auspiciously aligned. Rosy the Riveter and her colleagues were churning out those thousands of planes the president had ordered, and now the military desperately needed pilots. So the armed services promoted a novel program to help supply the need. The Civilian Pilot Training Program, which had been operating since 1939, was greatly enlarged and renamed the War Training Service. The WTS served as the screening program for potential aviators. In addition to pilots, the program produced mechanics, technicians, and radio operators. For would-be fliers, the WTS offered sufficient training to obtain a private pilot license at government expense. The military contracted with scores of civilian aviation operators across the country to provide fundamental pilot training using light planes. The program also weeded out unsuitable candidates, generally raising the quality of new aviation cadets. Graduates would enter military service better prepared for the intense training required to fly more sophisticated military aircraft.

Bruce felt he was the perfect candidate. So in the fall of 1942, during the war's grimmest phase, he walked confidently into the local Army Air Force recruiting office (the U.S. Air Force did not exist as a separate branch of the armed services until after the war). After duly filling out the paperwork in his uniformly neat handwriting, Bruce proceeded to a thorough physical exam. For prospective fliers, everything was tested, from head to foot. He sat in the Barony chair, which was spun around, and when it stopped, the subject was asked to walk. Like everyone else, Bruce stumbled, but he didn't fall or get sick. This test was supposed to determine something about a person's sense of balance, but Bruce regarded it as more of a hazing ritual. Other tests were more comprehensible, and each phase of the physical seemed to prove him a well-fit specimen — until that most crucial of all assessments for would-be pilots: the eye examination. This phase of the testing covered visual acuity, eye balance, depth perception, and color blindness. A deficiency in any of these faculties would be cause for rejection.

As it happened, the eye chart presented a certain problem — Bruce couldn't quite discern some of the letters. This meant he lacked 20-20 naked-eye visual acuity. Which meant he was out. No ifs, ands, or buts.

But Bruce was not so easily discouraged. The very next day found him at the local Naval aviation recruiting office. Maybe he thought the eye test would be different there. Or maybe he thought a good night's rest would improve his vision. Whatever the case, he subjected himself to another round of interviews, forms, and physical probings until he stood once again before those cryptic rows of progressively smaller letters that would spell his fate.

Bruce squinted, but the tiny letters would not resolve. He made excuses. He said he hadn't slept well. He pleaded for another chance. And amazingly the examiner agreed. Then providence intervened; the examiner was briefly called out of the room. Bruce seized the opportunity to whip out a pencil and pad from his pocket. He scribbled down the eye chart's nonsense arrangement of letters. That night he memorized each line — forward, backward, and even vertically down and up.

The next day the examiner found that Bruce's visual acuity had miraculously improved. Skeptical, he asked Bruce to read line 6 backwards. No problem. So he was in.

*　*　*

Prospective Naval aviation cadets were tracked into the WTS through the so-called V5 Program. While being processed, Bruce was asked to designate his top three choices for where he would like to undergo this initial training. Believing this request to be a humane effort to keep trainees reasonably close to home and make things generally more convenient for everyone involved, the young man listed three Ohio locations. The Naval bureaucracy then processed the information in accordance with its own inscrutable criteria and promptly dispatched its newest enlistee to the most suitable training facility.

Boise, Idaho, was not one of Bruce's top three choices. In fact it was about as far from any of them as he could get. But when all was said and done, he found himself billeted in a Boise Junior College dorm and eating at the school cafeteria. The V5 boys took flight training at Floating Feather Airport in Piper Cub J-5s. Bruce's instructor was Leona Bump, a graduate of famed stunt pilot Tex Rankin's aeronautical academy in California.

"I really was kind of scared of flying," Bruce admitted years later. Then perhaps realizing this wasn't the kind of confession one might expect from a man who had spent most of his life in the air, he explained: "I'd never thought that much about being a pilot. I was much more interested in being an engineer. But flying was the best thing I could be doing at the time."

The program at Floating Feather consisted of 25 hours of flying time — basic instruction leading up to a solo, some cross-country flying, and an introduction to aerobatics. Leona was a good instructor, and she put her students through the paces. She made sure they learned to do spins. Bruce hated spins.

But he learned well. In November 1942, Bruce made his solo

flight without incident. He landed and stepped out of the plane, smiling broadly. Leona approached and congratulated him. Then she said: "Now you go up there again and stay in sight of the airport. I want you to do a spin to the right and a spin to the left."

Bruce's heart sank. "Alone?" he asked.

"Alone."

"Now?"

"Now."

At that moment, Bruce might have preferred to sit in the Barony chair for a couple of hours or even crawl through a trench with bullets zipping overhead, but he got back into the Cub as ordered. At the proper altitude, he cut the throttle, eased back on the stick, and watched the air speed drop. The plane's nose went up. The air rushing over the wings slowed and began to buffet the airframe. As the stall broke, Bruce pushed the right rudder pedal and held the stick back. The nose fell and the world swirled. The wings creaked and air rushed around the cabin, but Bruce concentrated on what he was doing: stick full forward, rudder to neutral position. The Cub entered a straight-down dive, and Bruce pulled back to level. The process wasn't really so bad if you knew what you were doing.

The newly initiated pilot: Bruce K. Hallock still high from his solo, Floating Feather Airport, Boise, Idaho, November 1942.

Those who have flown with Bruce over the years may view this timorous initiation as ironic. The man was known for giving passengers unexpected thrills and breaking the tedium of long flights with abrupt and dramatic maneuvers. During the 1980s on a trip from Texas to California, while flying high over a New Mexico bombing range, Bruce realized his three passengers were suffering from boredom. Outside the desert stretched into a featureless haze. The cabin was warm, and we in the backseat were dozing off to the engine's throbbing drone. Looking out the window, Bruce said: "Oh, there's the target!" Suddenly the Navion's nose pointed straight up. Then the plane went over in a hammerhead stall. We were diving vertically, and now — yes — everyone saw the target rushing toward us. We were headed for a perfect bull's-eye marked in the sand. With plenty of altitude to spare, Bruce pulled out smoothly and set the Navion back on course. Somehow the time passed more swiftly after that.

* * *

After proving to Leona Bump and the U.S. Navy that he could fly, it was time for boot camp — of a sort. The Navy wanted to shape up its new aviation cadets with an intensive preflight fitness and indoctrination program. So from Boise, Bruce was sent to St. Mary's College in Oakland, California, for three months of calisthenics, swimming, soccer, wrestling, boxing, obstacle courses, and running — all without an airplane in sight. The cadets also attended classes on naval history, etiquette, and hygiene — all the fine points an officer-to-be must learn. And, of course, they drilled. They marched to class, to mess, to and from the barracks, everywhere. Cadet pay was $75 per month.

Bruce said the workouts were relentless, relieved only by ingrown toenails, headaches, and visits to the dentist. Still he managed to excel at running, making a time of 2:20 on the half mile.

It wasn't all sweat and pain, though. At one point, a dance was held for the cadets, and a bus full of girls arrived from the college.

Bruce charmed one of the girls into taking a long walk in the woods. They returned to find the girls' bus had already left for town. Trouble.

The next day Bruce was called before the commanding officer for a proper dressing down. The CO made references to his possible future as "a tugboat captain." Much standing at attention in the sunshine followed. But he wasn't washed out, and the calisthenics went on and on.

Finally one spring day in 1943, the Navy deemed that sufficient pushups and sit-ups had been performed, and the cadets moved on to Livermore, California, for primary flight training. Here they were introduced to the Timm N2T Tudor trainer, an all-wood, low-wing monoplane; the Stearman N2S Kaydet biplane; and the N3N, a Navy-built trainer similar to the Stearman. All of these were open-cockpit, tandem two-seaters.

The instructor sat in front, the student pilot in the back. No radios were used, so communication was primarily through hand signals. The instructor had a mirror on his windshield. There was also the gosport, a flexible tube connected to a set of earphones that allowed the instructor to speak to the student. "It was a one-way deal," said Bruce. "You couldn't talk back."

Marine Lt. Hockaday guided the cadets through the stepped program of basic instruction: solo, aerobatics, and formation flying (in the Timms). The program was demanding, and at first Bruce was frequently nauseous. "Every time we took off, Lt. Hockaday wanted to turn upside down," said Bruce. "I couldn't take it. I was sick." He feared he wouldn't make it, but something kept him going (tugboat captain, indeed!).

They had a separate check pilot for each section of the flight instruction. The grading system required that the check pilot put an up- or down-pointing arrow by each cadet's name on a chalkboard. A down on part of the program meant the cadet would have to do it over — three more months of that particular skill. Three downs equaled a washout. Somehow Bruce never got a down in anything, not even aerobatics — which is not to say there weren't problems.

Bruce made some pals during this time, among them Tony Hume and husky redheaded Matt Hoff. One day the three friends were flying formation in three Timms. Matt had told the other two about an interesting canyon he'd seen at the edge of the practice area, and he proceeded to lead them there. In line formation, they descended into the canyon and marveled at the steep cliffs rushing by on either side. And then — oops! They realized a little late that they'd flown into a blind box canyon. Throttles were jammed forward and sticks pulled back. The 220-hp Continental radials revved, and three bright yellow planes zoomed up, barely clearing the canyon rim. Sobered by their narrow escape, the three cadets resumed their legitimate maneuvers. Then out of nowhere, a Stearman appeared alongside their formation. Whoever was in that biplane had witnessed their little escapade. And he was writing down tail numbers.

Above: Timm N2T Tudor trainer.
Left: Stearman N2S Kaydet.

The suspense didn't last long. The three errant flyboys returned to base, taxied to the hangars, and cut their engines. Even before they could lift themselves from their cockpits, the loudspeakers were blaring: "HALLOCK, HOFF, HUME! REPORT TO THE CAPTAIN ON THE DOUBLE!"

On the way over to the office, Matt and Tony agreed that they just had to lie to keep from washing out. Bruce said he had never done that before and he didn't know how. This elicited some rolling of eyes, but there was no time to argue.

In the captain's office, three "jackets" lay out on the desk. "Jackets" were the personnel files containing each man's complete record with the Navy from the day of enlistment. Bruce's even documented his problem with the girl and the missed bus in Oakland. The three culprits stood at attention while the captain dressed them down. It didn't look good, and Bruce assumed he was finished. "We never had a chance to lie," he said. But after a serious bawling out, the captain assigned the punishment—one week on the wash rack.

The planes on the wash rack were often in need of cleaning inside and out where pilots had lost their lunch. In spite of being grounded, the three had to pass all their coursework. After a week off flight status, they had to catch up with the class, which they managed somehow.

At graduation Bruce had 400 hours of flying time, about 150 of it in Stearmans. He'd also received an excellent introduction to the fundamentals of celestial navigation. By contrast, Army pilots sometimes were given as little as 150 hours of flying time before they were put in B-17s and sent overseas. Navy flight training was much better.

And there was more to come.

* * *

Throughout 1943 the war had turned ever more ferocious. British and U.S. heavy bombers were pounding Germany day and night—at great cost to both Allied fliers and the Nazi war machine. In the south, the invasion of Italy had commenced, and Mussolini's Fascist regime had given up in September, but the Germans were keeping the Allies from moving up the peninsula. And in the Pacific, the U.S. had undertaken an arduous and bloody island-hopping campaign against the tenacious Japanese foe.

No one knew how it would end, and one way or another, Bruce assumed he was headed for the thick of it. After graduating from basic training, he was allowed a brief visit home before he had to report to Beeville, Texas, to begin his secondary flight training. Toward the end of his leave, he paid a visit to his old friends at Wright Field. There he learned that a captured German Ju-88 happened to be headed for St. Louis in support of a War Bond rally. Bruce talked the pilot into giving him a lift in the sleek enemy fighter-bomber. From St. Louis, he caught a ride to San Marcos, Texas, aboard a more mundane C-45 (the Beech Model 18 or so-called Twin Beech), a type with which he would soon gain great familiarity. From San Marcos he hitchhiked (by automobile) down to Beeville.

The secondary flight training in Beeville focused on instrument flying and was conducted in Link trainers and SNVs. The Link trainer was a flight simulator, consisting of a crude airplane shape with a closed, opaque canopy. It was barely large enough for one person. It was mounted on a pedestal and swiveled and bobbed by means of a system of bellows and valves connected to the "pilot's" controls. The Link trainer simulated climbs, spins, and other maneuvers, and offered a safe and economical way to practice blind instrument flying. Small lights illuminated the control panel, and a "plotter crab" traced the trainee's make-believe flight on a table beside the instructor. The instructor could also add effects such as wind resistance.

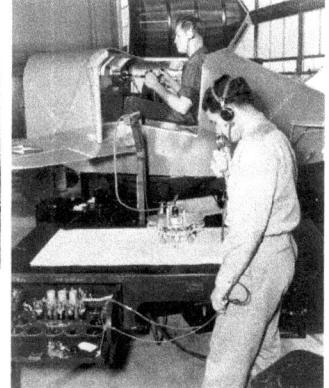

Above: Vultee SNV-1.
Right: Link trainer with plotter crab on table in foreground.

The SNV, on the other hand, was a real airplane. It was the Navy's version of the Vultee BT-13, a closed-cockpit secondary trainer used to introduce new pilots to more complex and powerful aircraft. Flying the SNV meant learning to deal with a variable-pitch propeller, radio communication, and radio navigation.

Beeville was a small town without much going on in the vicinity. So when the cadets got a day off — typically every eighth day — they wanted to go somewhere else. The most obvious choice was Corpus Christi, about 40 miles away. Like the others, Bruce hitchhiked to Corpus a couple of times and found the seaport town crawling with his Navy compatriots. So when he and a friend got a couple of days' leave around Christmas, they decided to get a little farther away. They hitchhiked north, bypassing San Antonio — which was known to be full of Army guys — and got dropped off in Austin, the state capital.

It was Christmas Eve, 1943. Wandering around downtown Austin, the two Navy fliers eventually discovered an event for servicemen over at the Driskill Hotel. Upon entering, the two were pleased to see that they were the only Navy guys present; the rest were Army. It was always good to stand out in a crowd.

The place turned out to be a local effort to provide servicemen with a homey environment where they could just relax, write letters, make phone calls, socialize, and enjoy some light entertainment. The woman in charge welcomed Bruce and his friend and handed them little gifts. Each gift included an address book with the name of the person who'd donated the item, the idea being that the serviceman would then have someone to write to as a pen pal.

At that moment Bruce became transfixed by a winsome young brunet singing to piano accompaniment. He asked the woman in charge her name.

"Enid MacPherson."

Bruce glanced at the name in the address book he'd been given. It didn't match. Too bad. He pulled out his pencil (which he had habitually carried since the experience with the eye chart) and replaced the name with Enid's. At the intermission, Bruce made his way over to the singer's side. Awkwardly, he introduced himself and complimented her on her enthralling soprano voice. Then he said: "I need a little help here. Can I get a phone number for this name?"

According to Bruce, Enid grabbed the pencil away from him and wrote down her phone number. It so happened that Enid had an eye for men who stood out from the crowd, and she'd noticed him coming in. "I thought he was a civilian," she said later. "He had on an overcoat, and he was outstanding — so much taller than all those other fellows from back East. The place was full of those little short guys."

Bruce admitted that when Navy men got dressed up they looked more like civilians and generally cut a more dashing figure than their Army counterparts. Anyway, despite the mutual attraction, Enid couldn't go out with him that night — she already had a date. So they made a date for the next day — Christmas — a big family potluck at an aunt's house.

The woman in charge of the hotel event had a list of private homes where servicemen could stay, and Bruce and his friend spent the night in a splendid old downtown mansion. The next day he showed up at the appointed hour on the doorstep of a more modest house on the north side of town. That first "date" included most of Enid's extended family, so Bruce learned plenty.

Enid was the only child of Eugene and Ruth MacPherson. The family had arrived in Austin from Missouri in 1939. They'd suffered in the Great Depression and had come to Texas in search of a better life. Austin offered fair weather, economic opportunities, and the University of Texas, from which Enid would soon graduate. She was also working full-time at nearby Bergstrom Army Air Field as a teletype operator. Her father made a living dealing in used cars and real estate, and her mother gave piano lessons and rented bedrooms in their big house on Red River Street. A number of other relatives had followed the MacPhersons to Austin.

Bruce found himself heartily welcomed by the boisterous clan. They talked about the war, President Roosevelt, and life in Texas, Missouri, and Ohio. Then Enid's Aunt Verna walked over to the bookcase and pulled down a tome titled *Hallock Genealogy*. All were astonished to learn that Enid's father's sister's ex-husband was related to some Hallocks. Bruce and his family were all listed in the book along with a host of long-lived New England folk, making him a distant cousin of Enid's cousins. Small world.

Cupid seemed to be working his wiles, and Bruce spent the evening with the MacPhersons. Enid even found a date for his buddy. But duty called, and all too soon Bruce was back in Beeville sweating under the hood of the Link trainer and learning the ways of the SNV.

Perhaps he did not guess that his romantic destiny had been sealed at that point. There'd been plenty of other girls — in Cleveland, in Dayton, in Boise, in California — but none he hadn't been able to leave behind. Maybe he thought he could just go on as before. But now he found himself irresistibly drawn to Austin. Every eighth day, Enid would have one of her father's cars (usually a LaSalle or Cadillac) ready to go. They roamed the Texas hill country (to the extent that gas rationing allowed), often winding up at St. Edward's University campus where they'd park on a hill overlooking the city and talk until after midnight. There was plenty to talk about; everyone had big dreams for after the war. Enid brought along an alarm clock and set it in the glove compartment so they wouldn't be out too late.

And when Bruce wasn't in Austin, the letters flew back and forth.

* * *

While Bruce's romantic options dwindled, the Navy actually offered him a choice. After his stint in Beeville, he was asked to state his preference among three possible career paths: fighter pilot, instructor, or transport pilot. Bruce rejected the fighter-pilot option because, as he put it, he couldn't possibly shoot down an airplane—and he didn't really relish the idea of getting shot at, either. As for teaching, he felt he lacked the disposition (later he would find this wasn't so). So he opted for transport. The Navy agreed, and it was off to multiengine school at the Corpus Christi Naval Air Station.

The standard advanced trainer for this phase was the twin-engine SNB (the Navy designation for certain versions of the Beech Model 18). In Corpus three variations of the SNB were used. All had Pratt & Whitney R-985-AN4, 450-hp radials, and Bruce and the other student pilot just flew whichever plane was available at any given time.

The SNB-1 Kansan (known to the Army Air Force as the AT-11) was variously used to train bomber crews, gunners, and navigators. It was set up to simulate the environment of the full-size bombers with a dorsal turret gun, a ventral tunnel gun, a bomb bay accommodating ten 100-pound bombs, and a plexiglass nose for the bombardier. To allow for internal passage into the bombardier's nose compartment, the airplane had half an instrument panel and no control column on the right side. Bruce said that overzealous gunner trainees were not above using the 30-caliber guns to strafe cattle while flying over remote stretches of south Texas ranchland.

The SNB-2 (AT-7) and SNB-3 (AT-7C)—both called the Navigator—lacked the armament of the SNB-1. Specialized for navigation training, these two models could accommodate an instructor and

Navy SNB-1.

three students with chart tables and instruments for each. A rotatable astrodome was commonly mounted atop the fuselage. The SNB-3 featured a higher gross weight and more complex avionics than the SNB-2.

The Army and Navy used these Beech Model 18 variants extensively. And it's probably no exaggeration to state that the majority of U.S. bombardiers, navigators, and multiengine pilots in World War II underwent training in these planes.

Bruce's three-month course in Corpus Christi included night flying, cross-country flying, and instrument flying. The instructors used the same now-familiar grading system of ups and downs. Bruce avoided receiving any downs. Graduating from each phase entailed a check flight with a senior pilot. Others dreaded these check flights, but Bruce had no problems with them. He was becoming more comfortable in the cockpit.

Of course there were more trips to Austin. During this time Bruce formalized his informal engagement with Enid by proposing on the steps of the Texas Memorial Museum beside the dramatic statue of raging wild mustangs. She accepted, but no date was set. The future was too uncertain.

On May 10, 1944, Aviation Cadet Bruce K. Hallock became Ensign Hallock and his pay practically doubled. He got his wings, and the Navy promptly shipped him off for more schooling — this time to Atlanta, Georgia, for a couple of months of advanced instrument training, again in SNBs and the cramped ground-based Link trainer. In the air, the training was conducted with the student "under the hood" while the instructor watched for traffic. Bruce's instructor was prone to nap during these flights, but on one particular day he did wake up when someone broke in over the radio with the news that Allied forces had landed on the beaches of Normandy. It was D-Day, June 6, 1944. General Eisenhower announced: "We will accept nothing except full victory." Hopes ran high, but there was still a hard slog ahead.

By late June, Bruce had moved on to Roanoke, Virginia, to learn to fly DC-3s. This was to be the final phase of his training. He was billeted at the luxurious Roanoke Hotel, set in the gentle mountains, with a marvelous dining room and refined appointments. Pennsylvania Central Airlines ran the pilot's school, training the military men under contract.

The letters to and from Texas continued, and in early July Enid (chaperoned by an aunt) paid a visit to Roanoke. The two women were on their way back from the wedding of a cousin. By this time, Bruce had acquired a gray, two-door 1939 Plymouth he called *Miss Genevieve*.

Bruce and the other raw Navy pilots received the benefit of excellent instructors with many hours of experience. He was very satisfied with this last phase and, in general, with all his training. An incredible year of first-class instruction had culminated with his joining the ranks of multiengine, all-weather pilots.

At this point, the Navy gave Bruce a few days' leave, so he headed home to Ohio. Enid came up on the train, and they met in Dayton and proceeded by car to Medina. Enid characterized this visit, during which she met the Hallocks and toured Bruce's hometown environs, as her "audition."

Ensign Hallock, May 1944.

Chapter 4

FLYING BOATS AND WEDDING BELLS

At long last the Navy was ready to collect on its training investment by putting Ensign Hallock to work. He was attached to the Naval Air Transport Service, Squadron VR-6, and ordered to report to Miami, Florida, for his first active duty assignment.

The Naval Air Transport Service had been set up in 1941 to provide rapid delivery of equipment, supplies, and personnel all over the world. It was basically a military airline and airfreight service. NATS Squadron VR-6 operated out of a seaplane base at Dinner Key in Miami. Pan American Airways had originally set up the facility for its flying boats serving South America. The Coast Guard also kept some sea-rescue planes there. VR-6 flew Martin PBM Mariners.

The Mariner was a large, twin-engine flying boat. It was originally developed as a patrol bomber, intended for use against submarines and other ships, and for search and rescue missions — so most versions were heavily armed. The airplane's distinctive profile featured a deep fuselage 80 feet in length and high gull wings spanning 118 feet. Fixed wing floats depended from long struts. The horizontal stabilizer was set with a dihedral angle matching that of the wing's gull roots, causing the twin vertical fins to cant inward. Bomb-bay doors were built into the engine nacelles.

The version of the Mariner used by NATS was the PBM-3R, which lacked armor and armament. Turrets had been faired over, and a reinforced floor, cargo doors, a hoist, and removable passenger seating had been added. Extra fuel tanks occupied the former nacelle bomb bays. The engines were Wright R-2600-12 Double Cyclone, 14-cylinder, two-row radials (identical to those used on the

B-25) turning four-blade Curtiss electric props, which changed pitch in the hub. Unlike later versions of the PBM, the 3R lacked an undercarriage; it was a true flying boat. To bring one of the planes up on land for servicing, a crew of near-naked sailors would wade and swim out into the water with two dollies the size of trucks. They attached this "beaching gear" underneath, and pulled the plane up the ramp with a tractor. VR-6 had two large hangars at Dinner Key. At the time he was there, Bruce recollected that the squadron had seven or eight of the Mariners.

Considering that a war was going on, it was a pretty good life for the airmen of VR-6 Squadron. They flew scheduled runs, operating like an airline. All the commanding officers were in fact airline pilots who had entered the Navy fully commissioned, without undergoing basic training. The PBM-3R's usual crew consisted of a pilot, copilot, flight engineer, navigator, and frequently a seaman second class to perform various chores. Their routes took them south, throughout the Caribbean and down the east coast of South America. They called at Guantanamo, Cuba; Kingston, Jamaica; Port-au-Prince, Haiti; the Dominican Republic; San Juan, Puerto Rico; Trinidad; Georgetown, British Guyana; and on down to Brazil, stopping at Belém, Fortaleza, Recife, and Rio de Janeiro. But

PBM-3R.

mostly they flew back and forth to and from Coco Solo Naval Air Station in Panama. All these far-flung Naval stations played a vital role in monitoring enemy ship movements and servicing the Allied fleets. The PBMs carried Navy brass, spare parts, machinery, and critical supplies, including Coca-Cola (bringing the empty bottles back on return flights). Sacks of mail were also important cargo. And a certain admiral in Panama, who preferred to have his collars starched in Miami, entrusted his laundry to VR-6.

Bruce grew curious about these foreign ports, but the crews were strongly encouraged to stay on the bases and not venture into the "native" parts of the cities. "We were being protected from VD and other dangers," he said. The entertainment provided at officers' clubs hardly assuaged his frustrated curiosity, and Bruce would later find himself repeatedly drawn south to these exotic locales.

But meanwhile the work itself proved engaging and challenging.

* * *

The Dinner Key station was the only facility on VR-6's seaplane routes that operated at night. Because the destinations lacked

Dinner Key, circa 1945. Five PBMs visible (two in hangars). Pan Am seaplane terminal at left.

lighted facilities, flights leaving Dinner Key would often take off at midnight in order to set down in Panama or other ports by daylight.

They would taxi out to the takeoff area through dredged channels marked by infrequent buoy lights. At certain points sharp turns were necessary to avoid reefs and other obstacles. Variable winds made turning difficult. The plane tended to weathercock. Later models of the PBM had reversible props, but the 3Rs did not; so the crews negotiated tight turns by briefly cutting one engine's magneto and then quickly flipping it back on before it died. The flight engineer would sit with his finger on the switch counting off fractions of seconds. It was a risky business. Having an engine shut down and being stranded out on the water in the dark with the wind blowing meant real trouble.

Once out in the deep-water takeoff area, the pilot lined up on the right side of a row of buoys spaced 500 feet apart. The wings had to be kept perfectly level to avoid dipping a pontoon on one side or the other. Normally, when sitting still, a seaplane rides with one wing pontoon slightly out of the water. When the plane is in motion, keeping the wings level is tricky, particularly at night.

Most of the destinations lacked facilities for beaching the PBMs, so the plane had to be moored to a buoy in the harbor. To meet up with the buoy, the pilot approached it upwind as the seaman second class leaned out of a hatch off the port side of the galley, which was directly below the cockpit. The flight engineer cut the engines off and on to keep the plane from moving too fast. The trick was to slowly run the hull right past the buoy so the seaman could grab it. If the seaman missed the buoy, the pilot had to turn quickly to avoid hitting reefs or other obstacles. Bruce admitted to scraping bottom once, resulting in the need for some minor repairs. His incident report cited "adverse wind conditions." When the airplane was moored overnight, a pilot, a flight engineer, and a seaman had to stay with her just in case a change in the weather called for quick action.

Another procedure requiring exacting technique was taking off fully loaded from a calm sea. The Mariner needed rough water to help it get up on the step. The problem was particularly evident at Port-au-Prince, where a confined bay required a circular takeoff run. Bruce would taxi in a circle to create a wake and gain speed, then double back across his wake and, by cross controlling (as in a slip), make the plane jump into the air — a neat trick.

Landing at night also involved precision and timing. The pilot had to line up on a long final, aiming just to the right of the first or second buoy in the row marking the landing area. Rate of descent and air speed were critical. The plane descended at about 200 feet per minute. Landing lights could not be used because they would cause glare from the water. The shifting geometry of the line of lighted buoys (a half-dozen or so in all) indicated the angle of descent. Altimeter and barometric-pressure readings given by the tower could not be relied on, as they were not accurate within five or ten feet.

So without benefit of landing lights and relying on the configuration of the buoys, the pilot would set up with a precise air speed and rate of descent. Then within about 50 feet of the water, the ground effect could be felt under the plane. Even in a strong wind, the air was always rather smooth. So when this cushion of air was felt, it was time to set her down and hope for the best. Key West served as an alternate landing harbor and was used on a couple of occasions because of weather or smoke from Everglades fires over Dinner Key.

Instrument landings involved a primitive and laborious procedure called "boxing the station." The crew would identify a commercial radio station in the area and fly directly over the transmission tower on a given compass heading (preferably one of the cardinal directions) while maintaining a set speed. The pilot would continue on this heading for exactly one minute and then make a 90-degree turn to the left. This heading would be maintained for another minute, whereupon another 90-degree left turn would be executed. Two more minutes of straight and level flight would be followed by yet another turn to the left and another two minutes of straight flight. One more 90-degree turn would bring the flight path parallel to (but farther to right of) the original course over the station. After two minutes on this final leg of the box, the relative position of the landing site could be plotted (with adjustments for wind speed) in relation to the known position of the broadcast station, and the pilot could begin the approach.

This challenging flying was exciting and fun stuff for a 23-year-old. But sometimes things got a bit too thrilling.

For a while VR-6 Squadron was assigned to assist with training students in celestial navigation. The PBMs would take as many as a dozen students plus instructors out from Dinner Key on 24-hour flights over water (made possible by those extra fuel tanks in the bomb bays). The chief navigator would bring a slip of paper up to the cockpit requesting a certain heading for a certain amount of time while his students took turns in the dorsal blister fixing their sextants on the heavens.

These missions required three flight crews, working eight-hour shifts. Bruce did not favor this kind of flying, mainly because he had trouble sleeping in the cramped bunks and would lie awake worrying about the airplane. And with good reason.

By regulations any flight of six hours or more included a meal. The PBM had a tiny galley, which could only seat two or three. So the men had to eat in shifts. The meals were usually steak. On one occasion, Bruce was dining below when the cooking grease ignited and flared up. The fire was quickly brought under control, but it was a frightening situation. The fuel tanks were not far from the galley, and the whole plane could have blown up within seconds. Bruce reflected that such incidents may have accounted for some of the mysterious disappearances of the planes over water.

Another scare occurred on a return trip from Panama, less than

200 miles southeast of Miami, near Andros Island (the Bahamas). Bruce was flying. His copilot, Lt. Henry ("Rosy") Rosenbaum, outranked him, but pilots customarily traded off time in the left seat so everyone could get his hours. It was midnight when they learned they were headed toward a massive frontal system. The plane was at 9,000 feet, just about maximum for the load they were carrying (empty Coke bottles, the admiral's laundry, etc.). So they couldn't fly over the weather; they just had to plow on through it.

The rain hit, and the airplane started bouncing around, thunder and lightning everywhere. Bruce described the PBM as very heavy on the controls. Sometimes in rough weather the physical strength of both pilots was needed to handle the plane. So Rosy was helping out. At one point, Bruce saw him bracing himself with both feet against the instrument panel.

Then the navigator yelled: "The port engine's on fire!"

Bruce looked out the window. A big fireball was playing over the engine nacelle. Even the propeller was alight. After their initial panic, the crew realized what they were dealing with — St. Elmo's fire, or its near cousin, ball lightning. Both phenomena are electro-luminescent discharges thought to be caused by the ionization of air inside a strong electric field, typically during thunderstorms. The bluish-white glow can look just like fire, but it behaves very differently. It doesn't actually burn or cause significant damage, but it can be very alarming. To this day, the physics of the phenomenon remain somewhat uncertain. And the behavior is totally unpredictable.

The "fireball" started moving in along the wing's leading edge. It shimmered and danced, maintaining coherence. When it reached the fuselage, the brilliant specter passed right through the windshield and entered the cockpit. It crackled and bounced about, blinding the crew. They couldn't see the instruments. Finally the bizarre visitor departed as it had arrived. Moving on out through the windshield on the right side, it followed the wing to the other engine. Then it just dissipated, as if snuffed by the driving rain.

The name *St. Elmo* is a variation of *St. Erasmus*, an early Christian martyr and patron saint of sailors. During rough weather, frightened seamen used to interpret the blue-white coruscations around the tops of masts as a sign of his protection. Whether or not the old saint's guardianship had been extended to these latter-day mariners of the sky no one could know. They were just glad to be done with his most recent manifestation.

They weren't in the storm for long—only fifteen or twenty minutes of real time—but the subjective time dragged on, with rain battering the windshield and violent turbulence rattling the airframe. Bruce later called it the worst he'd ever experienced. When they finally emerged from the tempest and saw some clear spots between lightning flashes, they found they'd been bumped up to 14,000 feet. And they were turned around, headed in the wrong direction!

They wrestled the big ship back on course and left the storm behind. After about an hour, the twinkling lights of Miami appeared against a starry backdrop. Bruce lined up with the buoys and set the Mariner and her shaken crew down on perfectly calm water.

* * *

The hazards of his work and continuing uncertainty over the war had given Bruce second thoughts about marriage. Realizing he could just vanish over the ocean, he felt "this was no time to be involved in a serious way with a girl." So in late August of 1944, without explanation, he quit writing to Enid. She waited about six weeks and then started things up again by sending him a note written on the program of a play she had attended. The play was *By the Skin of Our Teeth*. Somehow her impulsive ploy worked. Bruce got over his gloominess and resumed the correspondence.

By this time there were indeed signs of hope. Although some of the war's most brutal episodes lay ahead, Paris had just been liberated and the Germans were on the run. On the other side of the world, Japanese forces were slowly being ousted from their myriad Pacific strongholds. The war-weary nation dared to anticipate total victory, and Bruce K. Hallock indulged in his own little gesture of confidence in the future. He bought an airplane. Nine hundred dollars he paid for a used 1941 Aeronca Chief, which he christened *Aerobella.*

"I just wanted an airplane," he explained.

And it was as simple as that. Bruce's near-term, postwar ambition was to own an airport. As a career, military life did not appeal to him. And neither did he care for the idea of airline work. But he had become fond of flying. He wanted to be his own boss, and he really liked small planes of the type one person could fly and maintain himself.

Long term? At heart Bruce was a designer and builder, and tailless schemes continued to occupy his musings. One day he would build his own airplane. Enid MacPherson fully endorsed these aspirations, and pretty soon she began to figure into Bruce's plans again. So the exchange of love letters continued. And at last they set a date for late May.

U.S. bombers were now striking the Japanese homeland. Nazi Germany undertook one last-ditch offensive, resulting in the infamous Battle of the Bulge, which only delayed the inevitable. In the spring of 1945 the Third Reich collapsed. Victory in Europe was declared. And in Miami, Florida, a wedding was planned.

Victory celebrations were still in progress as trains carrying in-laws-to-be rolled out of Texas and Ohio. Like animated arrows inexorably moving across a world map in a newsreel depiction of the Allied assault on the Axis powers, the trains converged on their common objective. Enid had arrived earlier to establish a beachhead. She set up headquarters in the home of local relatives and began making preparations for the big day.

Meanwhile a brand-new law went into effect requiring nuptial-minded couples to wait three days after obtaining a marriage license before actually tying the knot. This measure was intended to curtail some of the quickie unions between inebriated servicemen and impressionable young women, endemic during wartime. Not having secured the crucial document earlier, Bruce and Enid were forced to contemplate for a while longer the wisdom of their plans while entertaining their just-arrived parents and relatives.

But the little hiatus failed to induce any second thoughts, and the rescheduled wedding day, May 29, dawned bright and cheery. Ruth MacPherson helped her daughter slip into a gown of white embroidered silk jersey. The bride's dark brown hair had been swept into a pompadour with wavy tresses falling to either side. The effect was complemented by a fingertip vale of tulle bordered by embroidered chiffon. A strand of pearls, a gift from the groom, encircled her neck. Enid had just graduated Phi Beta Kappa from the University of Texas under the prestigious Plan II program. She was a trained soprano with a golden voice. She was drawn to flying and yearned for adventure — but more than that, she wanted a family. She'd had many suitors, and now she'd picked her man.

Over in the bachelor officers' quarters at Dinner Key, Ensign Hallock cleaned his white shoes and put on his smartly pressed dress whites (fresh from the same laundry favored by the admiral in Panama). Looking in the mirror, he adjusted his white cap with its lustrous brass eagle over close-cropped auburn hair. Slim and well built, he stood six feet, four inches. (Enid had told him he resembled Joseph Cotton.) If he had made a good impression as a cadet in an overcoat on that fateful Christmas Eve back in Austin, Texas, he had nothing to worry about now. He flashed his winning smile, and a confident gleam lit up his blue-gray eyes. He had just turned 24. He was ready.

It was a small ceremony, held at Brian Memorial Methodist Church in Coconut Grove. Besides the two sets of parents and a few relatives, most of the other attendees (including the best man) were Bruce's Navy buddies. Pastor Albert Dale Haigler performed the ceremony. Beforehand he had advised the couple on domestic finances and the art of equitable quarreling. Bruce and Enid had politely endured the lecture, confident that their love and special affinity transcended such mundane concerns. Now before the altar, they made a fine-looking pair standing together at solemn attention —he with his perky epaulets and she holding her bouquet of gardenias. Their knees popped as they knelt. With the final *I do* and the kissing of the bride, the party adjourned to the Old Castle Inn for the reception. Photos were taken, and toasts were offered.

Military duties did not allow for a proper honeymoon, but Eugene MacPherson put up the extravagant sum of $9 to treat the newlyweds to a night at the posh Rooney Plaza Hotel on Miami Beach. All night long, a band down on the patio serenaded them with a lively rendition of "Rum and Coca-Cola."

* * *

For the nation, it was still a time of uncertainty and scarcity. But for the newlyweds, Miami in the summer of 1945 was a wonder-

Bride, groom, and both sets of parents, Miami, Florida, May 29, 1945.

land, and the privations only put a keen edge on the adventure. Housing was limited, and Bruce and Enid considered themselves lucky to find a small room — sans kitchen — near Dinner Key. Without a place to prepare meals, they ate out frequently. Even at a nice club like the San Juan with a live band, a fine dinner could be had for $1.25. Since restaurant meals were exempt from food rationing, the couple amassed a surplus of ration points, which they splurged on odd luxuries. A favorite was canned fruit cocktail (90 ration points) dumped over vanilla ice cream.

Gasoline rationing kept *Miss Genevieve*, the '39 Plymouth, relatively rested. But strangely aviation gas was not rationed. So instead of Sunday drives, they took *Aerobella* up for leisurely weekend flights. Enid would bring along the newspaper and read aloud of the worldly cares passing beneath their wings.

One pleasant Sunday in mid June they followed the coastline north and set down briefly at an airport near West Palm Beach.

Enid and *Aerobella*, rivals for Bruce's affection.

Enid, who was learning to handle the airplane, made the landing. After a stroll around the airport, they headed back toward Miami. About ten miles north of Fort Lauderdale, they noticed an inviting stretch of smooth beach. The capricious couple imagined this would be a nice place to go wading. With the long summer afternoon waning, Bruce circled the spot a couple of times and proceeded to land. The wheels touched, and the plane slowed rapidly. The sand was much softer and deeper than it had appeared from the air. Then with a jolt, *Aerobella* nosed over.

"Get out quick!" yelled Bruce.

Gasoline dribbled from the cap on top of the wing, but no fire ensued. And neither of them was hurt. But poor *Aerobella*'s nose was buried in the sand.

A couple of swimmers who had witnessed the mishap helped right the airplane. Bruce thought the propeller would be broken, but evidently the impact had stopped it parallel to the ground. Miraculously the only damage was a dent in the cowling just below the prop.

Bruce cleaned off the sand and started the engine. Then with the help of some other people who had gathered, he tried to get the plane rolling, hoping to take off. But even with boards under the wheels, the throttle all the way in, and people pushing, she just wouldn't budge.

Plan B was to wait for low tide and try to take off on the smooth, packed sand near the water. But with evening advancing, that course of action would have to wait for the morn. So Bruce and Enid put the covers on the plane and trudged off toward the nearby town of Pompano Beach, where they hoped to spend the night in a hotel.

It must be noted here that the young couple had embarked on this Sunday outing spectacularly unprepared for the adventure it had become. They had no provisions, little in the way of tools and equipment, and only the skimpiest of attire. Bruce wore casual khaki garb and a baseball cap, but no tie or Navy blouse—though his wings and bars were in place. Enid sported a bright red two-piece sunsuit, which had earlier delighted her husband but now seemed less than adequate against the evening chill and no longer quite appropriate for the occasion. A policeman gave them a ride into town, where they managed to dine on milkshakes and graham crackers at a drugstore, about the only place open. The policeman warned them against leaving their airplane unguarded on the beach. "Turtle gatherers roam the beach at night," he said. "They'll disassemble your little plane in no time."

So they decided to spend the night on the beach and accepted the lawman's offer to take them back there. They were dropped off on the little road running along the beach. In the dark they wandered through the thicket of bushes and vines down to the beach and, by watching the sweeping beam from a lighthouse three miles off, eventually found their plane. Later, in a letter to her parents, Enid confessed: "It was really pretty spooky there at night with the waves pounding and whistling wind."

They piled sand around and up over *Aerobella*'s tail to secure the airplane and create a windbreak for themselves. Then they removed the cushions and seat backs to make a bed, filling in the cracks with newspapers. A couple of the guys who'd earlier helped them with the plane were sailors from a nearby Navy gunnery range, and they returned with two very welcome blankets and a flashlight. Finally the pair bedded down, but the shifting wind and blowing sand kept them awake most of the night.

In the morning, the two of them managed to drag *Aerobella* down to the band of wet sand exposed by the receding tide. But it was too soft. Using it for a takeoff strip proved impossible. And now the tide was coming in again!

Just then six bathing-suit-clad fellows came up the beach and helped lug the airplane back up to dry land. These guys also turned out to be from the nearby Navy gunnery range. Bruce inquired about getting some assistance from their base, and they encouraged him to talk to the commanding officer.

So on to Plan C. After a quick visit to the gunnery range and a conversation with the amenable CO, Bruce and Enid returned with a truckload of sailors. Wielding axes and other tools, the men cleared a swath through the brambles and palmettos from the little road down to the beach. Then like a team of ants transporting a big bug, they carried the airplane over the remaining obstacles from the beach up to the paved road.

Bruce wanted to take off on the road, but there were obstructions—not all of them readily removable. So he taxied slowly along the paved surface, veering this way and that, as the sailors pushed bushes and young trees out of the way. Finally he brought the plane to a relatively clear stretch of road where the only problems were a large tree and some telephone poles. The sailors set to felling the tree while Bruce sized up the poles. Then after a brief rest, Bruce gave the sailors $5 for their beer fund and again asked Enid if she really wanted to hazard the takeoff with him. Largely concerned about her indecorous attire, she answered with a definite affirmative.

It would be a very short takeoff roll, and they would have to get airborne in the space between two telephone poles. The sailors broke off a few more intrusive bushes along the roadside. A couple of guys stationed themselves down the road to stop cars. Bruce pulled the prop through and the 65-hp Continental coughed to life. He climbed in. Safety belts were fastened and cinched. As a precaution, Bruce asked Enid to keep a bunched-up blanket in her lap. The sailors held the plane back while Bruce revved the engine to full speed. Then at his signal, the men let go and shoved on the struts. The tail wheel quickly left the ground. But suddenly a crosswind whipped *Aerobella* over toward the poles. Bruce dipped the opposite wing and zoomed up at the same instant. They were in the air—and just barely in the clear!

The guys on the ground whooped and hollered. Bruce and Enid exchanged triumphant smiles and uttered big sighs of relief. They circled back twice to wave to their rescuers.

Bruce had called his base from the gunnery range and made arrangements to have someone else take the flight for which he was scheduled that afternoon if he failed to show up by noon. But he made it back in time.

While Bruce was away on trips for the Navy, Enid kept busy washing clothes (in the bathtub), washing the car, mending clothes, and even mending the airplane's floor mat. She also wrote scores of letters describing the wonders of her new life. At some point she conceived the idea of writing a book "about my adventures with this crazy man I'd married." (That unfinished manuscript, along with her letters and diaries, eventually served as a rich source of material for this narrative.)

* * *

By this time, Bruce's younger brother Macy had also joined the Navy. Occupied with radar school in Biloxi, Mississippi, his duties had not allowed him to attend the wedding. But shortly thereafter he got a couple of days' leave. Wanting to visit his brother and meet his new sister-in-law, he finagled a ride to Miami aboard a TBM Avenger torpedo bomber (the same type that president-to-be George H. W. Bush had recently bailed out of on the other side of the world).

Macy's flight would land at an airfield used for Navy practice just north of Miami, and Bruce arranged to meet him there with *Aerobella*. Advance permission to land at the field was required because *Aerobella* had no radio. Bruce was cautioned to watch for traffic. Indeed, as he approached, he found a squadron of F4F Wildcats practicing touch-and-go's. "Navy pilots fly much tighter patterns than Army guys," Bruce remembered, "and it was hard to find an opening." But he managed to insert the little Aeronca into the landing pattern. When he touched down, he cut his landing roll short and scurried off the runway to let more Wildcats rumble by.

Then he waited. And waited. The sun was low and turning orange by the time his brother's TBM appeared. Macy crawled out of the belly gunner's blister, delighted with his first-ever airplane ride — but Bruce was more concerned about his brother's second ride. Daylight was fading, and *Aerobella* had no lights. Furthermore a night flight of Wildcats was about to take off. So if they were going to go, they had to get out of there fast.

Defying common sense, the brothers took off into the sunset. And as soon as they left the runway, the Wildcats took off and, one after another, roared past the unlit Aeronca. The Navy fighters disappeared, and *Aerobella* flew on over the darkening city. Brown's Airport, where Bruce kept his plane, did not have runway lights, and by the time they arrived, it was impossible to see the dark-soil strip. No landing was attempted.

Instead they headed for a nearby landing strip that Bruce knew was paved with crushed white coral, visible in the dark. Being a very basic little airplane, *Aerobella* not only lacked a radio and exterior lights, she also was without a cabin light or instrument panel lights. And since Bruce never *ever* flew her in the dark, he did not carry a flashlight either. But his brother had come prepared. So as Bruce strained his Navy-certified perfect vision to line up with the faint glow of the coral strip, Brother Macy lit one match after another, briefly holding the flickering flame up to the instruments to read off altitude and air speed.

No music ever sounded finer than the crunching of *Aerobella*'s tires on that coral landing strip. The brothers tied down the plane and hitchhiked into Dinner Key. The next day they fetched the car from Brown's Airport and drove out to the crushed-coral strip to retrieve *Aerobella*.

Perhaps lessons were learned from this little adventure. But Bruce was not finished showing off for his brother. That afternoon he had to go up for a training flight in a PBM, just a brief refresher run. So he asked the commander if he might take his visiting brother sailor along for the ride. The answer was "No." This seemingly negative response was not a major deterrent. "It was a pretty loose operation there," Bruce later recalled.

The PBMs were anchored in the bay, and flight crews were ferried out by motorboats manned by enlisted men. So Seaman Second Class Macy Hallock stepped aboard the boat without provoking any comment. Bruce checked with the other pilot going on the flight, and he had no problem with the "extra sailor" coming along; so all was well. Once they got airborne, regulations really flew out the window. Macy got to occupy the copilot's seat and take the controls as Bruce coached him through a couple of takeoffs and landings.

That was his brother's third airplane ride. For his fourth, Bruce took him over to nearby Opa Lacka Airport and checked out a Stearman biplane. Bruce proceeded to torment his little brother with every aerobatic trick in the book—loops, rolls, spins, etc. (maneuvers Bruce once dreaded). Only after he was satisfied with Macy's pallor did Bruce bring him back to earth. All in all the young radar man from Biloxi was shown a pretty good time at government expense.

* * *

The days of the big seaplanes were waning. More and more remote destinations were acquiring fully equipped airfields. And waterborne aircraft were expensive to operate and maintain. So one day the fliers of Squadron VR-6 were told they would no longer be flying the PBMs. They were switching over to R4Ds (the Navy's version of the DC-3). But before this changeover occurred, Bruce experienced firsthand a striking portent of the PBM's outmoded status.

Several VR-6 flight crews were ordered up to a Navy base in Virginia, where a number of well-worn PBMs had been gathered, ready for scrapping. The military had some qualms about disposing of these expensive assets in full view of the taxpayers. So to avoid difficult questions, the powers that be wanted the planes flown down to Panama where the deed could be done less conspicuously.

When he saw the plane he was assigned to fly, Bruce had a few qualms of his own. She'd seen some hard service and was now stripped to the bare minimum for her final flight. But she was certified airworthy, and orders were orders; so the reluctant crew took off and headed south. All went well enough until about an hour out from their destination. The port engine sputtered and quit. Even with the other engine running close to the redline, the plane wouldn't maintain altitude. The worried crew assessed the situation and made some quick calculations. They decided to stay on course, despite being forced to begin their descent a bit early. So the tired old PBM described a long downhill hypotenuse all the way into Coco Solo, Panama, and her rendezvous with destiny.

They landed on one engine, and the next day Bruce watched the airplane being towed into the junkyard. There engines and other salvageable parts were removed. Then everyone got out of the way. "They had one of those big cranes with the heavy ball on it," Bruce said, "and they'd come along and just bash it into the airplane. They bashed it from all different angles! They had a bunch of PBMs there, and I watched them doing this to several of them."

The war was reaching its culmination, and things were changing fast. For a short while, VR-6 continued flying their Caribbean and South American routes in R4Ds based at Opa Locka Airport in Miami, which shared a control tower with nearby Navy Masters Field. Then the squadron was informed that all personnel and equipment were being transferred to Squadron VR-7. And by the way, they were going to the Philippines.

Chapter 5

NEW HORIZONS AT WAR'S END

On August 6, 1945, the Atomic Age dawned over the star-crossed city of Hiroshima. Three days later, a second Japanese city experienced the same horrific daybreak. President Truman wanted to bring the war to an expedient end, and he saw the atomic bomb as an unfortunate but necessary means of achieving that objective. Indeed, within a week Japan accepted the Allies' terms of surrender, and hostilities ceased. (The actual instruments of surrender would not be signed until the following month.)

Meanwhile Bruce and Enid's time in Miami was coming to an end. With a pending overseas tour of indefinite duration, Bruce first wanted to pay a visit to his hometown, Medina, Ohio, with his new bride. He was allowed two weeks' leave before having to depart for the Pacific. So as Imperial Japan capitulated, Bruce and Enid readied *Aerobella* and set out on a cross-country odyssey.

They headed north, planning to refuel in Augusta, Georgia, but a large storm system forced an eastward diversion. Columbia, South Carolina, now looked like the most promising stopover. But the rain was still heavy, and fuel was running low, so when Bruce spied a big airfield just south of Columbia, he decided to land.

They soon discovered that the enormous 10,000-foot runways were accompanied by no other airplanes or facilities. *Aerobella* sat alone in the midst of a downpour on a sea of concrete. Later they would learn that the place was an Army auxiliary base, a practice landing field for planes from nearby Columbia Army Air Force Base.

Bruce took off his shoes and shirt and practically waded to the nearby little town of North. Enid got out and washed her face in a stream of water running down the runway. Soon enough Bruce returned happily toting a five-gallon gas can from a service station. Carefully shielding the wing tank's opening from the rain, he poured in the precious liquid. The rain seemed to be abating and some daylight remained, so they decided to continue.

Bruce lined up *Aerobella* on the more-than-adequate runway and proceeded to take off. But just a few feet off the ground, the engine sputtered and quit. Thank goodness for that vast stretch of pavement!

Suspecting a fuel problem, Bruce examined the gascolator. Yes, indeed, it was water — and not-so-clean water, at that!

Meanwhile, two Jeeps bearing MPs came buzzing down the long runway. The men were doing Sunday watch, headquartered in an abandoned farmhouse overlooking the enormous field. While Bruce and Enid drained the water from the fuel system, the helpful MPs went off and returned with a couple of jerry cans of gasoline. With the fresh gas, the engine ran but with a serious cough. So they drained, refueled, and tried again. But after a couple of minutes, the gascolator half filled with water.

With evening nearing, the MPs offered to let the wayfarers stay at their farmhouse headquarters. Bruce and Enid made their bed on the floor with a cot mattress and cushions from the plane. In the morning Enid improvised breakfast for everyone, cooking miscellaneous rations on the wood stove. No one went hungry.

After breakfast Bruce taxied *Aerobella* up to the farmhouse yard and drained the gas again. When he peered into the empty tank, he could still see water droplets. He wrapped a cloth around the end of a stick and swabbed it out. Then he mooched another three gallons of 70 octane from the Army. The engine started and ran smoothly, so Bruce hitched a ride into town to get more gasoline. At the service station, he told the man in charge about the can full of water. The chagrined proprietor explained that the can of alleged fuel sold to Bruce in good faith had earlier been returned to the station by a motorist who said he hadn't needed it after all. In truth the motorist must have actually used the gas and then filled the can with ditch water before bringing it back. Plausible enough, considering that gasoline rationing was still in effect, but a dastardly switcheroo with *Aerobella* as its ultimate victim. Anyway, the proprietor gave Bruce five gallons of fresh gas, and the travelers were soon airborne again.

In Columbia, South Carolina, they drained the remaining automobile gas and refilled with 80-octane avgas. In a letter to her parents, Enid documented the whole saga, referring to herself as "copilot and contact navigator." Evening found the couple snug in a Cleveland hotel bed.

* * *

The following day, August 14, was designated VJ-Day in commemoration of the victory over Japan. Across the country ticker tape swirled in the streets and total strangers embraced. Over Medina, Ohio, a little Aeronca came in low. It swooped down on a certain house on the outskirts of town. The engine revved, and the plane circled back to buzz the house again. A man ran out of the house and stood beside the road waving a red tablecloth.

Almost a decade earlier in an upstairs room of that house, a dreamy-eyed boy had paused while working on a model airplane. Gazing out the window at the straight stretch of Akron Road, he had imagined this very moment—himself at the controls.

The Aeronca lined up for final approach. It sideslipped over a bank of trees and set down on Akron Road's narrow strip of pavement, a wingtip whooshing perilously close to the man with the tablecloth. The plane continued rolling on down the road, stopping right at the highway intersection as a large truck roared past.

Bruce gunned the engine and swung *Aerobella*'s tail around, then taxied back up to the house. His stunned father gathered up the tablecloth and ran to meet the plane. "The war's over!" he shouted through the clatter of the engine. The propeller stopped and the doors swung open. "The war's over!"

Later Bruce flew the plane to a legitimate landing field, from which he took a succession of relatives and friends up for rides. While *Aerobella* was parked, FOR SALE signs graced her side windows. Enid believed the end of the war meant that Bruce would not have to go to the Philippines. But Bruce wasn't so sure. Once set in motion, the great ship of Naval bureaucracy does not readily change course. Many *ifs* hung in the air, and Bruce wanted to be prepared. He fully expected to own another airplane after leaving the Navy, but in the meantime he did not want the encumbrance if he were on the other side of the world.

Bruce and Enid's postmilitary plans included making Medina their home. To that end they spent some time scouting the area for prospective airport sites. The town already had one airfield, but with the anticipated postwar aviation boom, everyone assumed there was room for another. That dream, however, would have to wait. By the end of their stay in Medina, the couple had not found the ideal site — or a buyer for *Aerobella*. So they flew back to Florida, where the beloved Aeronca finally found a new owner.

* * *

Bruce's suspicions regarding his immediate future proved out. His squadron was still headed for the Pacific. So he and Enid pulled up their shallow Miami roots and said goodbye to their friends — and then to each other. Enid departed for Texas and Bruce for the West Coast.

All the personnel and equipment from the old Squadron VR-6 were shipped out to Oakland, California, for the trip overseas. While waiting to begin the next leg of the journey, Bruce received a tip from a serviceman who had just returned from the Philippines. "If you want to make some easy money," the man said, "take a bunch of little things like sewing machine needles, razor blades, and lipstick with you. They don't have this stuff over there, and it's real easy to sell."

Bruce's first reaction was: *Yeah, that's crazy*. But on the last day before leaving California, he decided a small investment in such goods wouldn't hurt anything. So he purchased a sack full of merchandise at a five-and-dime store and stashed it in his trunk.

Nearly 2,400 miles of open ocean lay between Oakland and Honolulu, the next stopover on the squadron's westward migration. So the fliers had to improvise to extend the R4D's normal 1,600-mile range. Several 55-gallon drums of fuel were loaded into the cabin and plumbed into the airplane's gas tanks. A seaman hand pumped the fuel from the drums as needed in flight. Once they arrived in Hawaii, the drums were removed because the R4Ds could then island-hop the rest of the way to the Philippines.

Bruce's chief memory of his week in Honolulu was of his one-and-only attempt at surfing. The sport looked easy, so he and a buddy rented boards and paddled out. All around them other surfers were nonchalantly riding the breakers, but the two beginners couldn't even stand up on their boards. Eventually they reasoned it might be easier a little farther out. So lying prone on the boards they paddled away from shore, unaware that the receding tide was assisting their efforts. With their awkward position on the boards restricting their view, the pair failed to recognize their predicament until it was almost too late. Then they spent hours paddling back against the tide. By the time they staggered onto shore, the surfboard shop had closed, and their backs were charred.

* * *

The Philippine Islands had been under United States rule since the end of the Spanish-American War in 1898. Japanese forces had occupied the islands from the beginning of 1942 until the spring of 1945, and the region had seen some of the most savage fighting of the war. Now U.S. forces were reestablishing their hold on that vast and strategically located collection of archipelagos. The Philippines would soon gain full independence as a nation, but meanwhile the so-called U.S. protectorate was serving as a hub for operations throughout the region.

Bruce's squadron was based on the island of Samar, where the men were quartered in tents. The cuisine consisted primarily of Spam. And the foul-tasting water could be made palatable only by mixing it with generous proportions of lemon concentrate.

Wartime privations had created acute scarcities in the Philippines, and all kinds of manufactured goods were now in high demand — especially those made of steel. The man in Oakland with the business advice had been right — particularly about the sewing machine needles. Before the war, the Singer Corporation had made its treadle sewing machines quite popular throughout Asia. Now people desperately needed new needles.

"You could go into downtown Cebu City and hold up a packet of half a dozen needles, and people would just start bidding," Bruce said. "Before long I realized I didn't need to hold up a whole packet. I just held up one needle at a time, and people would pay a dollar for it! I did a cash business. And the same with lipstick and razor blades and stuff like that."

Some guys would buy T-shirts from Ship Service (the Navy's equivalent of the Army PX) for about 50 cents and sell them on the street for $5. Each man was allowed only two shirts a week, so no one could make too much of a killing. "That was a little on the shady side," Bruce said, "but everybody was doing it."

Even a fine linen dress of Enid's that had inadvertently gotten into Bruce's trunk was swept away in the entrepreneurial typhoon. Enid admitted the dress "looked like an old gunnysack when it wasn't ironed," so Bruce probably didn't realize its true value.

The NATS mission in the Philippines was essentially the same as it had been in the Caribbean — Naval logistics support. Or as Bruce put it: "It was just an airline-type operation. We flew cargo and people on scheduled routes." Cebu, Manila, and other places where the Navy had bases in the Philippines were regular destinations. But the shifting priorities at war's end had resulted in a certain amount of chaos and confusion among the armed forces' support operations. And Squadron VR-7 found little demand for its services.

"We got over there and immediately wondered why we'd been sent," said Bruce. "So what to do? Set up a training program. As though we needed training in R4Ds!" Nevertheless the squadron went out on instrument training flights several times a week.

But there was still plenty of downtime.

Eventually attention turned to a number of Grumman F6F Hellcats parked at one end of the base. The formidable planes sat idle, their wartime duties done. Bruce discovered that officers of a

Samar, Philippines, fall of 1945. Left to right:
Al Jones, Bruce K. Hallock, John Baxter.

certain grade who held the necessary qualifications could check themselves out in one of these fighter planes. This process consisted of sitting in the cockpit for two hours and reading the aircraft manual. "Then they'd let you fly it around the field," Bruce said. So he did.

The Hellcat was already a legend. Its introduction to combat in early 1943 had helped tip the technological balance in favor of U.S. Navy aviators. Mindful of the fighter plane's renown, Bruce started the 2,000-hp Pratt & Whitney R-2800 Double Wasp 18-cylinder radial and took off. He didn't quite push the Hellcat up to its 370-plus-mph capability, but his short flight gave him a taste of what might have been had he chosen another path after basic training. The intense experience also left him with a new respect for the men who took these mighty machines into combat.

Curiosity also led Bruce to volunteer for a strange project involving a much smaller airplane. The Culver Cadet was a light, low-wing, single-seater with a tricycle landing gear. Several versions of the Cadet had been widely used during the war for target practice. The plane proved an appropriately fast and elusive target for fighter pilots and antiaircraft gunners to practice on. Sometimes gun cameras were used. Sometimes the Culvers towed target sleeves. And some were flown unmanned as radio-controlled target drones for live-fire exercises.

The project on Samar involved the version of the Culver Cadet designated the PQ-14, which had a 150-hp Franklin O-300-3 up front and a bunch of radio gear aft. The military wanted to refine remote-control techniques with an eye toward developing flying bombs and specialized reconnaissance aircraft. The exercise Bruce participated in called for transferring remote control of the PQ-14 from a ground crew to a pilot in a B-25 and then back to the ground crew. Bruce's job was not to fly the PQ-14, but to ride in it while others controlled it. He would be the so-called "safety pilot." If something went wrong, he would take over and save the Culver (and himself). Otherwise he was just along for the ride.

Bruce taxied the plane out to the end of the runway. As the B-25 lined up on a long final, the Culver PQ-14 started down the runway under full throttle. The ground crew, stationed near the runway, performed the takeoff and climb out. Bruce just watched as an invisible hand finessed the control stick. At the first sign of trouble, he was ready to flip the switch that would give him full control of the airplane.

Soon the B-25 came flying along behind him, and the ground crew transferred control of the Culver to the airborne crew aboard the bomber. Electronic controls clicked and buzzed as the remote pilot guided the Culver through a series of simple maneuvers. Warily Bruce monitored the airplane's performance. When it was time for landing, the pilot aboard the B-25 set Bruce up on a final approach and returned control to the ground crew, which landed the airplane.

Bruce did not particularly enjoy the experience. Even though he could have taken over at any time, he found not having control of the plane eerie and disconcerting.

Grumman F6F Hellcat.

Culver PQ-14.

* * *

The fighting in the recently liberated Philippine islands had been fierce. Manila, the capital, was considered the second most devastated city of World War II (after Warsaw, Poland). While visiting the base near Manila, Bruce and some buddies took a big troop-carrying truck called a "six-by-six" into town. At every turn they encountered scenes of destruction from the heavy bombing. The urban infrastructure had been wiped out. Craters and rubble left many roads impassable, and some were still blocked off. Driving the powerful all-wheel-drive truck, Bruce became perhaps more adventurous than prudent. A large puddle in the middle of one street didn't appear to be much of an obstacle, so he forged ahead. Water splashed over the wheels, and the truck began to sink before Bruce could stop. They were stuck in a bomb crater. Another truck soon came to the rescue, pulling out the stranded vehicle with a winch.

With the war finished, great quantities of military equipment were being disposed of in the most convenient manner feasible. At the Navy base on Samar, B-25s had been collected from all over the region. Bruce saw the planes lined up on a long pier that extended into the ocean. The engines and other salvageable components had been removed. One by one the bombers were pushed off the end of the pier into the water. On Samar and elsewhere in the region, tons of equipment were just dumped into the ocean, in some places creating the foundations for new reefs.

Of course the war itself had also generated a great deal of wreckage. Flying over the shallow waters of the Gulf of Leyte, Bruce gazed down on a vast graveyard of ships and planes. Only a year before, a major battle had raged for three days across these very waters. The Battle of Leyte Gulf had drawn in some 282 ships. Both sides had taken heavy losses, but in the end Japanese naval power had been decisively broken right there. "Masts stuck up above the water," Bruce said. "The whole bottom of the ocean was covered with ships." Some of the wrecks likely predated the recent conflict.

Bruce's time in the Philippines was short. In late October he was happy to learn that his service time plus other points accumulated for foreign duty, etc., now allowed him to muster out of the Navy. Many of the guys heading back to the States wanted to get home as quickly as possible, and they elected to fly. But Bruce thought: "Boy, I'd gotten this far in the military and hadn't been killed, and I didn't want to fly one of these busted down airplanes home. They had B-17s and B-24s and whatever. Yes, I was scared to fly home in one of those war-weary airplanes." The other choice, of course, was to go by sea. Bruce thought a ship would be interesting. So he found a berth aboard a crowded troop ship.

As an officer Bruce was stationed amidships, which didn't heave as much as either end. The weather was nice, and the food was fine. But he still got seasick—all the way back to the States. Somewhere in mid Pacific, something broke in the propeller drive assembly, and the ship had to proceed at half speed. (The airplanes weren't the only war-weary conveyances.) Their destination was changed from San Francisco to Point Mugu, about 65 miles northwest of Los Angeles, where repairs could be made. Meanwhile Enid had driven out to San Francisco. So after landing at Point Mugu, Bruce hitchhiked up to San Francisco to reunite with his wife.

* * *

Bruce had come through World War II in pretty good shape, especially considering the devastation the conflict had wrought in so many other lives. He had lost a cousin. Other families had suffered far more. For better or for worse, the war changed just about everything. It broke some, while others benefited in odd ways. Many found themselves on wholly different paths than they might have taken had the world not turned upside down.

During much of the time he was in the Navy, Bruce had tried to secure reassignment to work that he felt would be more in line with his interests. He had applied repeatedly for transfer to either the Naval Aircraft Factory in Philadelphia or the Naval Air Station Patuxent River, Maryland.

The Naval Aircraft Factory had been in operation since World War I. It had built a few airplanes—most notably an early patrol flying boat and the N3N primary trainer—but it served mainly as a test and cost-evaluation facility for aircraft submitted by private industry.

The Patuxent River air station had been designated the center for naval aviation testing at the beginning of World War II. Bruce characterized the facility as the think tank of naval aviation design and experimentation with a mission similar to that of Wright Field's, but on a much smaller scale. In June 1945, the Naval Air Test Center was made a separate organizational entity from the air station itself.

Bruce felt his talents, qualifications, and enthusiasm were well suited for this type of work. But it was not to be. The Navy, for its own peculiar reasons, had wanted him flying transports, and the experience he had gained doing so would lead to an extraordinary career.

Meanwhile more uncertainty—and adventures—lay ahead.

Chapter 6
AIRPORT SCHEMES AND GRANDER DREAMS

Like many men coming out of the armed forces at the end of World War II, Bruce King Hallock had big plans. Postwar expectations ran high—especially in civil aviation. Pent-up aspirations could finally be given free reign. Bruce's career objectives now looked something like this:

1. Get an airport and open a flying service.
2. Design and build airplanes.
3. Contribute to the advancement of civil aviation.

Starting a family and generally enjoying life—especially through flying—would also fit somewhere into this picture.

During the war, Bruce had made a start at each of these ambitions. His purchase of the Aeronca Chief had been his entrée into the world of light planes, which in turn got him interested in airport operations as a possible means of making a living doing what he loved. The airport and associated flying service could serve as a stepping stone, an interesting way to support himself while working on his long-range goals.

The dream of designing and building airplanes stretched back to his college days when he first began to draw up detailed plans. His stint at Wright Field had further stimulated this urge. His ideas were constantly evolving. Onto magazine pictures of conventional airplanes, he habitually penciled swept wings, always imagining new shapes and refining his ideas. The big quarter-scale model he had finished just before entering the Navy was the precursor to a full-scale design he called the HT-1 ("HT" standing for Hallock Tailless), a four-place, single-engine pusher. The HT-2 he envisioned as a larger twin engine. The HT-3 would be—well—something else.

Postwar aviation was shaping up as an exciting and dynamic business, and Bruce believed he had something to contribute. Throughout the war he had continued working on his book, a definitive technical investigation of tailless aircraft. The ambitious work was divided into four parts:

I. "History of the Tailless Airplane"—which surveyed significant tailless efforts from the early Dunne types on up through contemporary designs. Bruce had amassed an impressive collection of photos for use as illustrations in this portion.

II. "Aerodynamics and Design Consideration"—which included chapters on airfoils, stability, wingtip arrangements, control surfaces and systems, flaps and other lift and drag increasing devices, fuselage shapes, and submerged power plant and propeller installations.

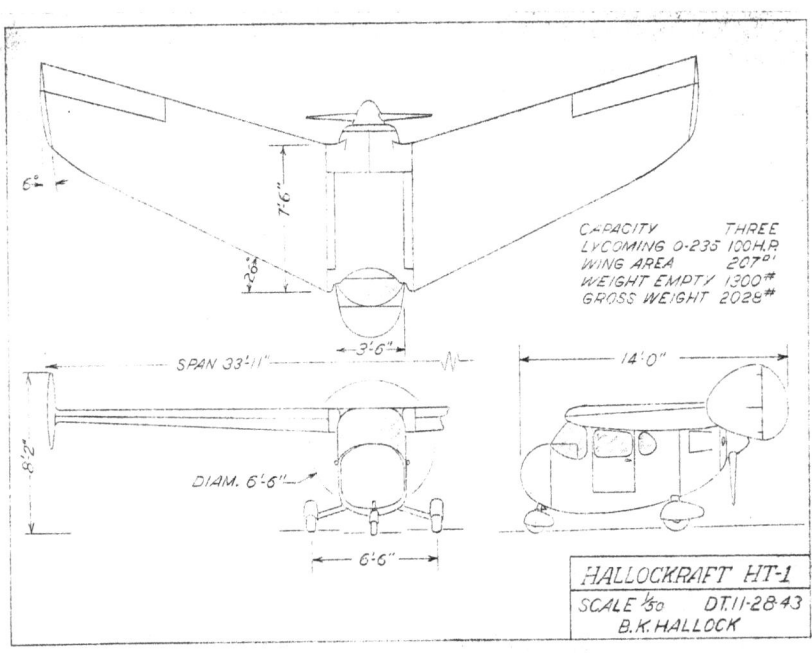

Early plan for HT-1, originally conceived as a 3-seater with passenger in back sitting sideways.

III. "Comparisons of Hypothetical Tailless Designs with Conventional Airplanes"—which considered the relative merits of tailless bombers, fighters, transports, cargo planes, and personal aircraft as contrasted with their conventional counterparts. For this portion of the book, Bruce had sketched various conjectural designs to illustrate his points.

IV. "Advantages and Disadvantages of Tailless Airplanes" — which included discussions of general aerodynamics, drag, the wing-fuselage interface, and structural considerations.

Essentially it was intended to be the book Bruce had yearned for as a young engineering student, but could not find—a comprehen-

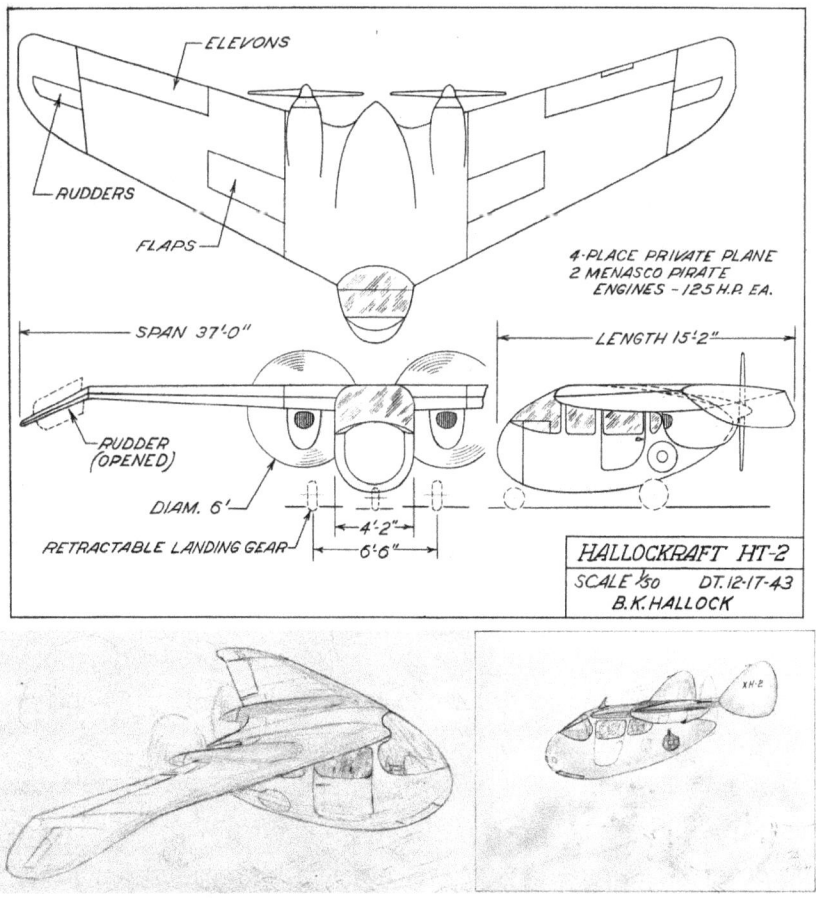

Early concepts for the HT-2.

sive examination of tailless aerodynamics. He continued working on the manuscript into the early 1950s. Although the book would never see publication, his exhaustive research had turned him into something of an expert on the subject and an enthusiastic proponent of the tailless configuration. Bruce's gift was to view the ever-evolving field of civil aviation in terms of his special perspective and thereby conceive new possibilities. He was full of ideas.

But first he had to start earning a living.

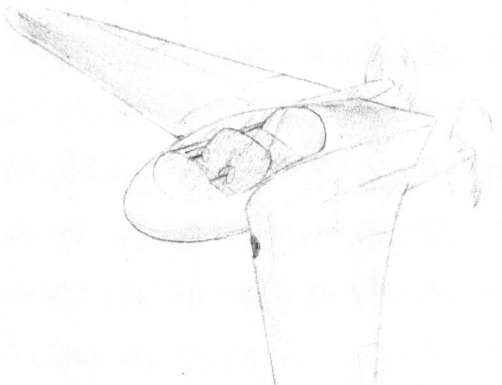

Hypothetical tailless concept by
B. K. Hallock intended as book illustration.

* * *

After Bruce mustered out of the Navy in California at the end of 1945, he and Enid drove back through Texas and ultimately on to their new home in Medina, Ohio. Along their circuitous route, they stopped at practically every little airport to take the pulse of postwar aviation and get ideas for how to proceed.

They also wanted to buy a new airplane, but high postwar demand and the awkward transition to civilian production made many manufactured goods hard to get. Finally, though, in February 1946, Bruce and Enid took possession of a brand-new Aeronca Champion. They kept the plane at a small field called Fenn's Corner. Although barely adequate, the short strip with utility wires along one side would have to do until a better location was found.

Bruce had to sideslip when landing. To wash the airplane, he and Enid fetched water in a bucket from the restaurant across the street.

The Champion was fun. Enid christened her *Flossie*. She could take off in as little as 250 feet. But the plane had bitten $2,295 out of their nest egg, and Bruce wanted it to start earning money right away. So he offered rides. He and Enid erected a fifteen-foot banner: RIDE IN NEW 1946 AIRPLANE $2. And the people came. Many locals—including three children who squeezed together into the rear seat—came out to Fenn's Corner for their first airplane ride. For an extra dollar, Bruce offered a special "thrill ride." On really good days *Flossie* earned over $50—on lousy days, nothing. Usually the take was somewhere in between. Bruce also put the word out that he would fly anyone or anything anywhere for a fair price. A local newspaper needed a critical part for its broken printing press, and a railroad strike prevented a timely delivery. Bruce flew over to Chicago Midway Field and picked up the part. That got his picture in the paper and helped generate publicity.

He also earned some money ferrying new Taylorcrafts to dealers around the country. By mid 1946, the factory in Alliance, Ohio, was rolling out 30 new airplanes a day. Bruce and others flew in loose formations of as many as ten planes to Denver, Atlanta, Kansas

The Champ at Fenn's Corner, Medina, Ohio.

City, and other major cities.

That summer Bruce took advantage of the Servicemen's Readjustment Act of 1944 (better known as the GI Bill of Rights) to obtain his flight instructor's rating so he could offer yet another service. But he also realized that a bigger airplane held the key to greater profits. In August, with help from his father, Bruce purchased a new 1946 Stinson 108 Voyager 150. Considering the high demand for personal planes, he also saw the Stinson as a smart investment. In fact the airplane-resale market was looking so good that, within a month, he acquired another new Stinson Voyager, a factory demonstrator, with the intention of profiting on its resale.

California seemed like a good place to sell one of the Stinsons. So Bruce found a passenger who wanted to fly west and took off. Unbeknownst to him and the woman sitting beside him, another, nonpaying passenger had also climbed aboard. The journey went well enough at first. Then somewhere over Arizona, Bruce had to fly high to get over the weather. The cold, thin air must have disoriented the stowaway. Bruce felt something moving on his leg. He looked over at his passenger, but she was just gazing out the window and keeping her hands to herself. Then he glanced down. A mouse was climbing up his pants.

In one motion, Bruce grabbed the befuddled critter and, sliding the window open with the other hand, tossed it out. The woman

Bruce's "fleet" of Stinson Voyagers.

never knew why Bruce suddenly opened and closed the window.

Bruce failed to find a buyer for the plane in California, so he got more serious about the air charter business. His advertised rate was 13 cents per mile for round-trip flights. This was his whole-plane rate, regardless of the number of passengers. So, for example, three people could fly the 780-mile round-trip to Philadelphia and back for $100 (rounded off). For an overnight layover, a whopping $10

New -- AIR PASSENGER CHARTER SERVICE

1946 FOUR-PASSENGER STINSON "VOYAGER"

★ Business and Professional Trips
★ Vacationing, Fishing, Hunting

Tomorrow is Here

- **Very Low Rates**

   At new rates, lower than anyone has heretofore offered this type of transportation, you may fly anywhere. Consider the time saved and compare the prices attached to this sheet with other methods of transportation.

- **Safety**

   You will be flown in a new spin-proof postwar Stinson airplane inspected and licensed by the Federal Government and flown by a Government certified ex-Navy transport pilot. The plane carries liability insurance of $15,000.

- **Convenient, Personalized Service**

   No schedule; leave when you like. Fly direct to practically any city or small town. Save precious time and arrive clean and refreshed for your appointments. Three passenger seats are available - two small children may take the place of one adult. You will ride on soft upholstery, in a quiet, heated cabin listening to the football game or music from the radio speaker in the cabin ceiling. One trip will prove to you that flying is the essence of travel.

The Week-end Becomes a Week

BRUCE K. HALLOCK

PHONE: 2-9363

116 WEST NORTH STREET   MEDINA, OHIO

Advertising flier for Bruce's air-charter service.

surcharge was added (which was probably all profit, as Bruce likely found an empty couch in the pilots' lounge or curled up on the backseat of the plane).

There was some business, but Bruce certainly wasn't getting rich. Also he still hadn't found a better piece of real estate for his airfield. And by late fall, the weather began to hinder flying more often than not. Bruce and Enid had been considering moving operations to Texas — at least for the winter — and now the prospect looked more attractive than ever.

After a couple of reconnaissance missions down to Austin, the move was made. And by this time, a baby was on the way.

* * *

In Austin, Texas, Bruce made the acquaintance of Charles Quist and his sister Mary. The siblings owned a struggling little flying service based at St. Edward's Airport just south of town. The words "AUSTIN AERO SERVICE" ran above the door of the sole hangar. Charlie had been an Army Air Force pilot, and Mary Quist had flown with the Women Airforce Service Pilots (WASP) during the war. The brother-and-sister team had one airplane, which they both used for instruction. Only a couple of other light planes were based at the airport. Bruce entered into a partnership with the Quists, and his three airplanes gave the enterprise a big boost. His Aeronca Champion served as a basic trainer, and they used his Stinsons for advanced training, air charter, and rental.

St. Edward's was a sleepy little airport. Sometimes Bruce arrived early to find cows had taken over the grass landing strip during the night. The listless beasts scarcely noticed as he started up the Aeronca. With no one else about and the windsock hanging limp, Bruce just took off from the taxi strip and zoomed over the heads of a couple of puzzled bovines. The airplane banked steeply and headed back low and fast over the herd. This got their attention; some of the beasts began sauntering off. The Aeronca turned around and lined up for another full-throttle pass. Now the cows were moving a little faster, scattering in several directions, some actually trotting. For good measure, Bruce made another high-speed pass and then landed. The runway had been cleared, and the airport was opened for business.

Winter turned to spring with surprising swiftness in Central Texas, and the business bloomed like a field of bluebonnets. Ex-servicemen were using the GI Bill to take flying lessons. People were buying airplanes, and the winged population of St. Edward's Airport multiplied.

And as Austin Aero Service helped mint a new generation of fliers, a new generation of Hallocks also came along. In May 1947, Enid gave birth to Bruce Glen, followed twenty months later by Donald Macy in January 1949. Enid and the babies became part of the airport's cast of characters.

Airports have a way of attracting the ambitious and adventurous,

Ready to take off on a vacation trip to Mexico in late 1948. Left to right: Eugene MacPherson, Ruth MacPherson, Bruce Glen (1½ years old), Enid M. Hallock (pregnant with Donald Macy), and Bruce K. Hallock. Austin Aero Service hangar in background. Note baggage in foreground. Everything and everyone pictured went into the Stinson.

and Austin Aero Service certainly had its share of these types. Young men enamored of flying machines, young men seeking thrills, young men wanting to impress young women, and a few young women with their own motives all found their way to the airport.

A fellow named Rocky Parker was one such ambitious and adventurous individual. With no more than a fourth-grade education, he'd lied about his age and joined the merchant marine during the war. Two ships had been sunk out from under him. He'd wanted to become a fighter pilot, but his lack of education thwarted that dream. He had joined the Air Force anyway, and served for a while as an airman at Bergstrom Air Force Base, not far from St. Edward's Airport.

Rocky began hanging out at Austin Aero Service. He didn't have an airplane or much money, but he'd earned a pilot's license on his own and loved to fly. Cheerful and eager, he was willing to do just about anything for a chance to go up. He'd sweep the floor, mow the grass, wash planes—anything to ingratiate himself with the owners of the airplanes. At the time, no one could have guessed that Rocky Parker would eventually go on to a long and illustrious career as an international airline pilot.

Bruce and Enid became fond of the bright young man, and Rocky soon got his way. The days were busy, but when the work was done, Bruce and Rocky were not above a little horsing around with the planes. Enid tells of the two guys taking up the Stinsons and engaging in mock dogfights, buzzing low over the field, and generally performing stunts that would have gotten Naval Cadet Hallock busted out of flight training in an instant. "It scared me to death!" she said.

But Enid herself didn't mind indulging in a little excitement from time to time. She soloed in the Aeronca Champion and continued to put in flying time in that airplane. And her diaries contain exuberant descriptions of the sheer joy of flight. "On the way back from [*Robert Mueller*] Municipal Airport we did a beautiful loooooooooooooop!" she wrote.

Perhaps this author's earliest memory is of approaching St. Edward's Airport in a Stinson Voyager. I sat on my mother's lap. Suddenly my father reached over and shut off the magnetos, saying: "Okay, we don't need this anymore." The drone of the engine was replaced by the eerie swoosh of air around the cabin. We spiraled down to meet the grass strip. The wheels rattled on the uneven ground, and our momentum carried us right up to the hangar.

* * *

For many of the denizens of St. Edward's Airport, these would be remembered as the good old days. The tight little community of regulars spent long hours working on their planes, flying, and just shooting the breeze while the babies napped on a scrap of linen fabric. "You could always tell who was there by the cars in the lot," said Enid. The Hallocks' gray Plymouth might be parked between a bright yellow Jeep and a flashy Cadillac. And after dark the same set of folks often mingled socially. Lifelong friendships were forged. Matt Roberts started flying at Austin Aero right after the war and

Enid piloting the Aeronca Champion with Bruce (probably) in the back seat, St. Edward's Airport, Austin, Texas, circa 1948.

went on to a distinguished career in both military and commercial aviation. Over the ensuing decades, he and Bruce would often cross paths. Jim Newman was another regular who remained a lasting flying buddy of Bruce's.

But perhaps the most colorful of the airport's characters, the one everyone still talks about, was Buster Davis, a high-rolling gambler and well-known pimp. With his big straw hat and pink Cadillac convertible, Buster certainly looked the part. He lived at Evelyn's Place, one of the cathouses on South Congress Avenue. He'd once shot and killed a man who was gunning for him, but he was well liked around the airport. He usually had a wad of large bills in his pocket. One time he loaned Charlie Quist the cash to buy an airplane on the spot. Buster had learned to fly (after a fashion), and he owned a couple of planes at different times, one of which he cracked up there at the field, nosing it over in the mud.

Although flight instruction, charters, and rentals represented the bread and butter of Austin Aero's business, these basics weren't so dependable that other opportunities could be ignored. The publisher of the local Austin newspaper was persuaded that small planes would be an effective means of getting the daily paper to its more remote readership. So for a period of about six months, Bruce and some of the other regular fliers at Austin Aero assumed the role of flying paperboys.

Before dawn Bruce would pick up several bundles of papers and head for the airport. He flew a route out to Burnet, Llano, Blanco, and other small towns, dropping off bundles at local airfields. And along the way he also delivered individual papers to remote farms and ranches. These were wrapped up securely and dropped from the air. The customers enjoyed the novelty of the airplane flying over low and slow just to deliver their paper. "We had very few complaints," Bruce said, "even when the paper landed on the roof or in a tree."

Sometimes Bruce used the Aeronca Champion for the deliveries, but he preferred the Piper Cub with its flop-down door, which made it easier to toss out the papers. For the bulkier Sunday edition, he had to use the larger J-5 Cub Cruiser, which lacked the flop-down door. The economics of this venture were pretty marginal, but Bruce said it garnered some publicity for Austin Aero.

The Stinsons and other airplanes stayed busy. Sometimes when a plane was expected to return after dark, smudge pots would be set out to outline the runway. Automobile headlights were also pressed into service for predawn takeoffs. People attending out-of-town football games were frequent charter and rental customers. Others were more unusual. A polio nurse needed to get to Corpus Christi in a hurry. Two cowboys in full regalia hired Bruce to fly them to San Angelo for a rodeo. Knowing they would have to perform as soon as they landed, the cowboys placed their ropes down close to the airplane's heater to keep them limber.

The business grew and underwent changes. Austin Aero took on another partner, Lenny Marks. And Bruce eventually left the partnership but stayed on good terms with the others and continued flying out of St. Edward's Airport. They even continued sharing airplanes. Charlie Quist had purchased an Aeronca Sedan, a four-passenger plane comparable to the Stinson Voyager. So Charlie and Lenny were now technically in competition with Bruce, but there was plenty of business to go around in those early days.

The usual complement of postwar light planes flew in and out of St. Edward's. On any given day, one might see Aeroncas, Pipers, Taylorcrafts, Stinsons, Ercoupes, Interstates, and Luscombes. Surplus military planes also showed up, especially trainers of all kinds, including a brand-new Fairchild PT-19 that Charlie Quist sold to Buster Davis, the high roller. At one point three BT-13s (identical to the Navy SNV that Bruce had trained in) were based at the field.

Right after the war, Charlie Quist had bought a UC-78 Cessna Bobcat for $2,800. Whatever plans he had for the plane hadn't worked out, and the Bobcat sat out in the elements for a couple of years totally uncared for. The fabric rotted, and people began "borrowing" parts from it.

Finally one day Bruce told Charlie: "You've got to get rid of that thing."

"I know," Charlie sighed.

"Well, I'll give you $10 for it," Bruce said, half joking.

"Sold!"

Bruce handed over the money and walked out to take possession of his new airplane. He was as surprised as everyone else when both Jacobs R-755 radials, which hadn't been run for years, started right up. The Bobcat was in no condition to fly, but Bruce taxied it over to the hangar on its flat tires. He had no plans to restore the plane; rather his scavenger's eye saw it as a source of parts. Some he sold (the propellers alone brought $75 apiece), and some he kept for a special project.

Bruce clowning around with his bargain Bobcat. It started right up! Note both engines running in lower photo.

* * *

The aeronautical engineer in Bruce had been stirring for some time. Since before the war he'd wanted to build a marketable light plane. He'd been working on drawings, and in early 1947 he began construction of the prototype. His current design closely resembled the large *Baffle Bird* model he'd built while working at Wright Field. In fact this full-scale effort would incorporate refinements that had emerged from his research and experiments with tailless models dating back to the 1930s.

When he began construction, he hadn't yet decided on a name. Officially it was the HT-1, but people just called it the *Big Baffle Bird*. That moniker, along with some of the plane's features, would change more than once as the project progressed. But the basic concept remained constant—a tailless pusher capable of competing in the emerging four-place private-plane market. Bruce wanted to keep the design simple and affordable.

But he also wanted to stay abreast of changing trends, and one idea that got his attention early on was *roadability*. In aeronautical parlance, roadability is a feature that allows an airplane to be converted by its pilot for use on public roadways. Waldo Waterman had tried to commercialize the concept in the 1930s with his Arrowbile, but his efforts (and those of other early pioneers) had not panned out. However, after the war the idea of roadability took on new life. With the booming private plane market, it was assumed that customers would demand more versatility. Airports were not typically convenient to people's ultimate destinations. And parking an airplane at an airport could be expensive and inconvenient. So the postwar vision of the future conflated the airplane and automobile as never before. Popular magazines routinely pictured hypothetical airplane-car hybrids driving in traffic or parked in garages, their wings neatly stowed alongside garden rakes and the kids' bicycles. Roadability seemed a natural development, the logical next step in the popularization of aviation. And Bruce K. Hallock was one of its prophets. In 1950 he wrote an article (unpublished) titled "The Roadables are Coming," in which he concluded:

> A roadable airplane will have the utility necessary to make short flights between cities practical, even while airports remain miles from town. Such is certainly not true with current private planes, regardless of their speed. When a reliable and not too expensive roadable airplane has been developed, then, and not before, a mass market in private flying will be available.

But despite new materials and technologies, many challenges remained. From an engineering perspective, the marriage of automobile and airplane is an unnatural one. The design requirements of the two vehicle types conflict in several areas. The most obvious incongruity lies in the differing basic shapes. Wings tend to stick out, while cars require a more compact body plan. Foldable or re-

Fulton Airphibian. Above: Car module detached from wings and tail. Below: B. K. Hallock tries out a prototype Airphibian, Cleveland, 1948.

movable wings present a host of practical problems. And other, less-obvious considerations—such as control systems, drive trains, and even human-factors engineering—also confront the designer with conflicting priorities.

Bruce surveyed contemporary efforts and gained an intimate appreciation of the problems involved. At the 1948 Cleveland Air Races, he met Robert Fulton and rode in his Airphibian. Fulton's two-place car module could be detached from the conventional airplane module. With the propeller removed, the six-cylinder Franklin aircraft engine supplied power to the wheels. The Civil Aeronautics Administration eventually certified the Airphibian, but financial difficulties thwarted mass production.

Another prominent contribution to the roadability effort was Moult Taylor's Aerocar. It featured a front-wheel-drive car module powered by a Lycoming aircraft engine. This was mated to a flight module, which included the wings and rear fuselage. A drive shaft connected to a propeller mounted behind the tail. The wings could be folded back along the detached rear fuselage, and the whole package was then towed as a trailer behind the car module. The Aerocar also obtained CAA certification but was not a commercial success.

Bruce realized that most designs compromised either aircraft performance or roadability—or both. A relatively nice car typically came at the expense of a mediocre airplane and a hefty price tag. A good example of this tradeoff could be seen in Theodore P. Hall's ConVairCar. In 1949 the Consolidated Vultee company poured a considerable sum into the project, hoping to market a good car that could also fly. As a car it was satisfactory, but as an airplane the ConVairCar was not a great performer.

Bruce noted that all roadable designs fell into two broad categories — those that required the removal of the flight equipment (wings, etc.) before being driven as an automobile (the Airphibian and the ConVairCar, for example) and those that could carry their flight equipment with them as they plied the roadways (like the Aerocar). The former offered the advantage of a relatively unencumbered automobile module more able to function as a normal ground vehicle. The latter offered the advantage of not having to store the flight equipment at the airport and always having it available if the need arose to drive to another airport. Bruce favored the more integrated, take-it-with-you approach.

Taylor Aerocar.   ConVairCar.

"The ultimate roadable plane," Bruce wrote, "will be a good family car that can sprout wings and be readied for flight by pressing a button." But such a goal, he readily admitted, would not be attained in the near future. Meanwhile he did not expect that people would give up their present-day automobiles for a combination vehicle that lacked good roadway performance. Instead he proposed a good airplane that incorporated just enough automobile qualities to offer convenient transportation to and from the airport. It would not be a replacement for the family car, but an uncompromised airplane that possessed added utility — a roadable aircraft as opposed to a flying car. This set Bruce's design apart from most other contemporary efforts. To the casual observer, the roadability feature of his airplane would not even be apparent — except perhaps in the name that he'd chosen for it and painted on the nose: ROAD-A-PLANE.

Bruce further believed that his tailless pusher configuration lent itself well to roadable conversion. He would take a cue from Moult Taylor and devise a system for pulling the folded wings behind the fuselage like a trailer. But unlike Taylor's Aerocar and most other roadables of the time, the Road-A-Plane would be free of any complex and weighty mechanism for transferring power to the wheels. Instead the prop would spin between the folded wings to propel the vehicle down the road.

Because the project competed with the demands of earning a living and raising a family, more than a decade would pass before the finished airplane would take to the air. But Bruce persisted.

The fuselage took shape—first in the backyard of the West Austin duplex where Bruce and Enid lived in 1947 and early '48, and then in the hangar of Austin Aero Service. He started with a keel that would run from the nose bulkhead back to the rear firewall. It was made of one-inch-thick spruce faced on all sides with eighth-inch, three-ply mahogany. Working with the keel turned upside down, he attached a series of wood formers and stringers that defined the fuselage's rounded undersurface. Longerons connected the outer ends of the formers to define the bottom edges of the cabin. Then the bulkheads were attached, and the upper fuselage was assembled. The keel protruded slightly through the cabin floor. Welded chrome moly steel tubing formed the main spar and its

Road-A-Plane display model showing right wing and rudder folded and ready for the road, and left wing extended in flight position. Propeller clearance would be worked out later. Bruce carved the model from solid balsa in the late 1940s.

supports, but the fuselage was mostly wood, with aircraft plywood the predominant covering.

To save time and money, Bruce incorporated some fittings and detail pieces salvaged from other airplanes, but the Road-A-Plane was not just thrown together from used parts. The design was distinctively original. The fuselage and wings were built from scratch. Still Bruce was constantly on the lookout for useful hardware. The Cessna Bobcat he'd salvaged contributed its nosecone, a rudder, and some other fittings. The nose gear, control wheels, and control system hardware came from an Ercoupe. Bruce cut down the wing struts from a Stinson Reliant. The shock struts for the main landing gear he took from a BT-13. The main landing gear itself came from a wrecked Stinson Voyager—as did the wheel pants, door handles, gas tank, cowling and grills, and spinner. And the engine and seats used in the Road-A-Plane were procured in a most remarkable manner.

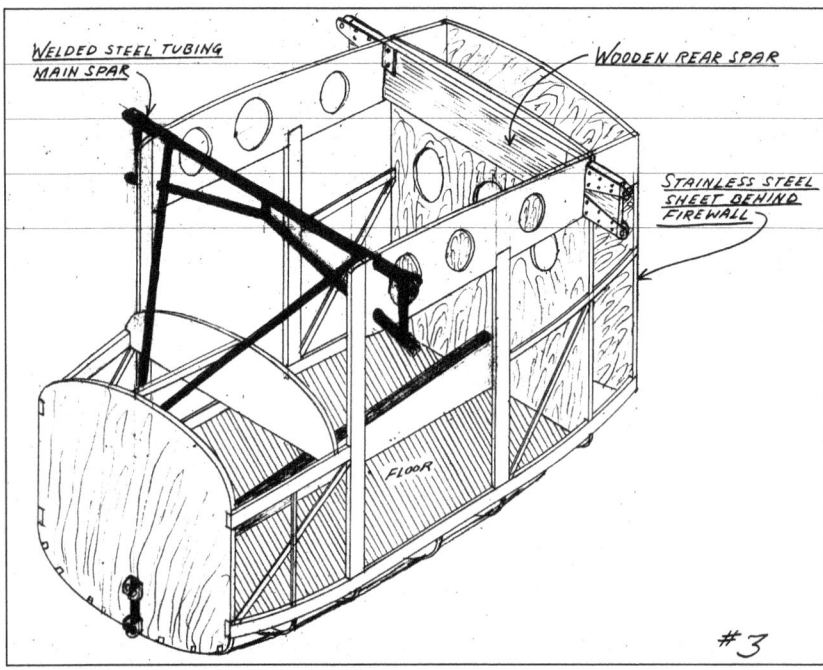

Road-A-Plane fuselage construction.

* * *

In part to explore the prospects for charter flights south of the border and partly just for fun, Bruce and three other fellows took Charlie Quist's Aeronca Sedan down to Mexico's Yucatán Peninsula and into Guatemala. On the return trip, they refueled in Tampico and then headed north for Brownsville, Texas. But after barely more than half an hour in the air, the engine started acting up. Since the 260 miles of desolate coastline between Tampico and Brownsville offered no decent place to land, they turned around. Upon returning to the Tampico airport, they found a hole burned in one of the pistons. The problem was more than they were prepared to deal with at that point, so the four travelers returned to Austin by bus. Then Bruce, Charlie, and Bill Kimbro (a friend) gathered their tools and flew one of Bruce's Stinsons back to Tampico.

They changed out the Sedan's damaged piston and got the plane ready to fly. Charlie decided to take it up for a test flight by himself. Soon after he cleared the end of the runway, the engine quit. He turned around and tried for a downwind, dead-stick landing but couldn't quite reach the runway. He plowed through a stockade and crashed into a railway maintenance shack. Propelled by fear of an imminent explosion, Charlie bounded over the stockade. No fire erupted, but Charlie had suffered a broken leg, an injured hand, and facial lacerations. He was rushed to a nearby hospital. The Sedan and the shack were totally wrecked.

A day passed, and it became apparent that Charlie was not being well served by the local health care system. He'd been moved from the hospital to a hotel. Bruce went to see him and discovered he hadn't even been cleaned up. He wanted to take Charlie home, but the authorities wouldn't allow it. The problem seemed to be that the maintenance yard and shack he'd demolished were the property of the Mexican government railway. Charlie was being held under house arrest until the matter could be settled. Negotiations were attempted, but to no avail.

Fearing a long and painful (for Charlie) bureaucratic nightmare, Bruce and Bill decided to act on their own. Early the following morning when monitoring of the detainee was thought to be most lax, Charlie's two friends helped him limp out of the hotel. They handed the clerk some money and told him that if anyone asked they were just going to get breakfast and would be right back. Actually they had arranged for a local lady friend of Charlie's to pick them up and drive them to the airport. Bruce slipped some cash into the palm of the man who was watching his Stinson and explained that they only needed to gas it up. The three gringos then piled into the plane and took off without clearance. They flew into Brownsville without a flight plan and told their story to the U.S. Customs officers, who simply replied, "You were lucky to get out of there."

Once back in Austin, Charlie got proper medical attention. His leg had to be re-broken, as it hadn't been properly set.

Meanwhile, Bruce couldn't let that wrecked Aeronca Sedan just sit; it contained many salvageable parts — including the engine, which he wanted for his project. So at the first opportunity, he removed all the passenger seats from his other Stinson Voyager and flew down south of the border by himself. The Mexicans had moved the wreck from the crash site into a hangar where it was now impounded. Bruce's claim of ownership fell on deaf ears until he slipped some cash into the right hands. He hired the airport mechanics to dismantle the Continental O-300 engine and wedge it into the back of his Stinson. He also loaded in as much other salvageable stuff as he could, including the wheels, the seats, and all the instruments.

Flying back to Texas, he decided to bypass Brownsville, the usual point of entry. "There was no way I wanted to make an excuse for having that engine in the airplane," he said. So he flew straight to Austin and unloaded his cargo.

But he still had to account for himself with the U.S. Customs Service. So the following morning he reinstalled the passenger seats in the Stinson and headed for San Antonio, which had a customs office for processing international airline flights. Swinging wide and approaching from the south, he radioed that he was arriving from Mexico and needed to go through customs. The air-traffic controller directed him to the appropriate hangar.

He taxied up and shut off the engine. Immediately uniformed officials surrounded the airplane. "Don't open the windows or doors!" ordered an officer. Another man came running up with an insecticide sprayer. Bruce was forced to remain in the airplane while they fumigated it inside and out. Then they set up a perimeter of red ribbon around the plane and put a guard on it. Bruce was led away for questioning.

"Why didn't you land at Brownsville?" they wanted to know.

"Well, the weather was bad, and I had to go around the fog. I couldn't make it into Brownsville, and I knew you had customs in San Antonio. So I landed here. Is there a problem?"

The problem was that they just weren't accustomed to processing private flights in San Antonio and didn't quite know how to react—hence the overreaction. Bruce ended up explaining his story over the phone to someone in Washington, D.C. When it finally became clear that he wasn't a criminal and that his airplane was sanitary and free of contraband, they let him go. But this wouldn't be his last brush with federal authorities.

* * *

By late 1949, changes in the GI Bill had led to a drop-off in the demand for flight instruction, the mainstay of Austin Aero's business. This downturn, along with other economic factors, spelled the end for the once-thriving enterprise. The people and planes that had kept the little airport buzzing flew elsewhere. The old windsock fell to tatters. Errant breezes rattled the hangar doors, sending ghostly echoes through the empty building. And on the runway and tie-down area, weeds and lush grasses lured back the cows.

Chapter 7

BUSH PILOT AND FISH MONGER

Even before the demise of Austin Aero Service, Bruce had begun to cast about for other income-producing schemes. More and more his thoughts had been turning south of the border. One of the more unusual charter jobs he had undertaken while flying out of St. Edward's Airport was a trip down to Belize City in British Honduras. His passengers were a man and a woman and their little girl, along with many of their household possessions. The woman was from British Honduras, and she and her husband were moving down there to join her family in the burgeoning lumber business. At the time chartering a flight was the most expedient way to get to the isolated Central American colony. So in addition to his three passengers, Bruce loaded the Stinson Voyager with considerable baggage and other miscellaneous items, including a baby carriage, a mop, and a case of canned milk.

In those days the backwater British colony was a far cry from the hot tourist destination it would later become as the independent nation of Belize. "They had a boat from Tampa, Florida, once a month," Bruce said. "And the Mexican airline flew in there once or twice a week. Except for private flights, that was it. The place was way off the beaten path."

British Honduras was wedged in between Guatemala to the west and Mexico's Yucatán on the north. Sparsely populated beaches and small coastal islands called *cays* dotted the Caribbean coast, while dense jungles and swampland dominated the interior. Belize City, the colonial capital, boasted a population of only a few thousand. The so-called city was little more than a collection of wood-frame buildings — largely unremarkable, except that much of that wood was mahogany. "Even the fences were mahogany," Bruce said.

Fine hardwoods were only one of the resources awaiting exploitation in British Honduras. The ocean also held riches. Every morning the old swing bridge spanning the Belize River would be hand-cranked open as the fishing fleet moved out to sea. Then in the evening, the bridge would again open for an hour or so as the boats returned. This ritual cut Belize City in half for extended periods each day, so the fire department routinely stationed one of its two fire trucks on each side of the river to ensure that the wooden buildings on both sides of town had protection.

Among the bounties brought in from the sea was succulent rock lobster, which sold for absurdly low prices. Bruce sampled the crustaceans and was impressed. Back home he asked around at some Central Texas restaurants, and the show of interest started him scheming. With a bigger airplane, he might make a bit of money hauling fresh lobster north, where it would sell at a premium.

The idea appealed on several levels. Since his days in the Navy, Bruce had felt the allure of remote and unsophisticated places, especially Latin America. When things at the airport had become frustrating, he had occasionally voiced a half-serious desire to "just run off and bum around South America." His Mexican escapade culminating in the salvage of the wrecked Aeronca Sedan's engine had sprung from this impulse. And before that he and Enid (pregnant for the second time); their infant son, Bruce Glen; and Enid's parents had packed themselves into a Stinson Voyager and flown into Mexico's interior. These brief trips had inspired further research into the region and whetted Bruce and Enid's appetites for grander adventures. So a business plan that involved flying down to Central America proved irresistible.

Bruce made another research trip to British Honduras. He flew alone in one of his Stinsons. He contacted a prospective supplier and brought back a few lobsters on ice. Then he began shopping for a suitable airplane and decided that the most practical and affordable was the Noorduyn Norseman.

The Norseman was a large, single-engine cargo plane that had served the Army Air Force as the UC-64. Like other war-surplus planes, Norsemans were now widely available on the civilian market. They appeared regularly in the publication *Trade-a-Plane*, and Bruce checked out several. He sold one of his Stinsons and scraped together the necessary funds. Eventually he contacted a man in Brownsville, Texas, who had four Norsemans for sale.

The man's name was Penney, one of the owners of the J. C. Penney Company. He had acquired the fleet of Norsemans with the idea of starting up a small airline serving the Rio Grande Valley and South Texas. The venture hadn't worked out, and now he just wanted to get rid of the planes. The price seemed right, so Bruce and Enid flew down in their Stinson with a friend. Bruce picked out the best-looking of the bunch and handed over $4,000—less than half the asking price of a comparable Norseman he'd looked at in Dallas. "If he'd had the money," Enid said, "he would have bought two of them." Bruce and Enid flew their new Norseman back to Austin with their friend following in the Stinson.

The Canadian-built Noorduyn Norseman was designed for use in the rugged northern bush country. Its 600-hp Pratt & Whitney R-1340-AN-1 incorporated an oil-dilution system to improve cold-weather starting. The distinctive bowlegged landing gear could be fitted easily with wheels, floats, or skis. To enhance takeoff performance, the ailerons deflected downward by 15 degrees when the flaps were deployed. Large doors facilitated the handling of bulky cargo. During World War II, the UC-64 Norseman had served as light transport for Allied forces around the world. With a wingspan of 51½ feet, it was among the largest single-engine airplanes ever mass-produced. The roomy cabin accommodated up to ten passengers.

The plane that Bruce purchased, NC59888, had been nicely appointed with comfortable seats and mahogany paneling. He removed the seats and installed four large sheet-metal "lobster bins," custom built by an Austin roofing company. Bruce based the Norseman at Browning Aerial Service at University Airport, but he also flew out of Haile Airport, a small airfield that flourished for a time virtually underneath the final approach to Robert Mueller Municipal Airport.

Noorduyn Norseman NC59888 poses with new owners, Bruce and Enid.

* * *

Early in the morning of November 22, 1949, Bruce took off on his first lobster run. To maximize profits he had loaded the Norseman with certain high-value, easy-to-carry items that he knew would be popular in the remote British colony. He refueled in Tampico, Mexico, and flew on southeast across the Bay of Campeche and the trackless jungles of the Yucatán Peninsula, arriving at the Belize City airport by day's end. In all it was a journey of some 1,270 miles, a very full day of flying at the Norseman's cruising speed of about 145 mph.

He had called ahead and arranged for a local fisherman to meet him at the airport the following morning with a load of lobsters. Meanwhile the merchandise that Bruce had brought sold right off the airplane. U.S. cigarettes, magazines (especially *Playboy*), ham, mustard, and fresh tomatoes all proved very popular. "People knew I was coming," he said, "and they came out to the airport." A small crowd gathered around the airplane, and people vied for the goods. It reminded him of selling the sewing machine needles in the Philippines. And upon learning that Bruce would be making regular trips to Belize City, some people asked if he could procure certain hard-to-get items for them in the United States. So he took orders for things like refrigerator parts and medicines to bring back on his next trip.

In the morning the lobsters arrived live at the airport. The fishermen dumped them in a pile and twisted off the tails, throwing away the front parts. The high-value tails went into the Norseman's lobster bins, and Bruce covered them with chipped ice.

By the time he took off, insufficient daylight remained to fly all the way back to Austin, so Bruce stopped over in Tampico. There he got into a taxicab and visited the local ice plant. The taxi returned to the airport loaded down with bags of ice, and Bruce made sure the

Bruce's Norseman at Belize City Airport, 1950.

lobster tails were well chilled for the night. The following morning he landed in Brownsville to pass through customs. Then he flew on to San Antonio, where a hotel had arranged to buy 500 pounds of his cargo. In Austin he sold more to other restaurants.

The lobster tails for which he'd paid 10 cents a pound in Belize City brought 50 to 60 cents a pound north of the Rio Grande. It seemed he had a good thing going. No one else was exploiting this particular opportunity. The riches of British Honduras just weren't in other people's awareness. So more trips followed.

To ease the monotony of the long flights, Bruce usually invited someone to accompany him. On one trip, his father-in-law, Eugene MacPherson, served as "copilot." On the way down, they stopped in Campeche, Mexico, which at the time was a thriving center for shrimp exporting. There were big freezers at the airport, and large cargo planes (mostly Douglases) arrived on regular schedules to haul shrimp back to the States. An umbrella-covered stall at the airport sold shrimp cocktails for 10 cents, and Gene ate three in a row.

Bruce had kept in touch with the family that he'd helped move down to Belize City in the Stinson, and he and Gene stayed at their large house with the mahogany picket fence out front. On the way back, Bruce and Gene cleared customs in Brownsville and flew on north. Although the weather was overcast, they hoped to make it into San Antonio, where the fine china of the Gunter Hotel dining room awaited most of his lobster tails. But as the Norseman flew on, the cloud cover pressed ever lower. Bruce wasn't flying on instruments; he was just following Highway 181 leading into San Antonio. This rudimentary form of navigation (visual flight rules) requires weather conditions sufficient to allow the pilot to control the aircraft and maintain separation with obstacles by relying primarily on what he can see out the window.

Finally near Floresville, Texas, Bruce conceded that visibility had deteriorated to the point where he could not proceed. Reluctantly he selected a straight segment of roadway free of obstacles, circled once, and set down without trouble. He taxied the airplane safely off into a driveway.

One of several motorists who stopped to see what was going on had a pickup truck, and Bruce hired the man to haul his perishable cargo into town. Gene accompanied the man and saw that the consignment was safely delivered. What didn't go to the hotel went into a commercial cold-storage facility. Then Gene proceeded to Austin via bus.

The airplane spent the night beside the highway, and Bruce stayed with his friend Rocky Parker who happened to live nearby. The next day, Bruce made arrangements with the highway patrol to temporarily stop traffic and allow the Norseman to take off. All in all the incident was pretty uneventful, although readers of the *San Antonio Express* were treated to a sensational and totally fictitious account in which the descending aircraft had narrowly missed a school bus.

Bruce enjoyed finding goods to sell, flying down to British Honduras, and being greeted at the airport by eager customers—but he didn't care for dealing with seafood. He worried constantly about spoilage, and selling the lobster tails took considerable time and effort. Most of his customers refused to order in advance. When he couldn't sell his haul right away, he stored it at a commercial ice house. San Antonio and Austin were his prime markets, but he also peddled his lobsters in Houston and Dallas. He wasn't a natural salesman, and being a fish monger seemed a far cry from his real objectives of designing and flying airplanes.

"I couldn't sell the lobster fast enough," Bruce said. "At one time I had a couple of thousand pounds in cold storage. I was getting behind on my sales. We didn't have much money, but we were eating lobster three times a day."

At last it came time to cut his losses, and Bruce advertised the Norseman for sale in *Trade-a-Plane*.

* * *

During this time, Bruce had continued working on the Road-A-Plane. Its fuselage was now mostly complete and itching for wings. He had installed the 145-hp Continental O-300 salvaged from the Aeronca Sedan. The engine spun a custom-made left-hand Sensenich wood propeller, for which Bruce had paid a $75 premium to have the backward jig set up. By early 1950, the wingless machine was whizzing through the streets of the South Austin neighborhood where he and Enid now lived. The dark-blue paint job was set off by yellow trim stripes.

The neighbors generally enjoyed the novelty, but the police were less enchanted. A puzzled traffic cop who got up the nerve to pull over the unlicensed vehicle told Bruce that he wasn't sure if there was a prohibition against such an unconventional automobile. So to solve the problem, he just said: "I'm going around the block, and when I get back, don't let me find you here." The policeman left, and the Road-A-Plane disappeared back into the garage — temporarily.

Enid, Bruce, and Road-A-Plane ready for the road but not for the air, Austin, Texas, 1950.

Road-A-Plane powered by Continental 0-300 on the streets of Austin circa 1950, the author in the copilot's seat.

* * *

Bruce devoted what time he could to his pet project, and to stay solvent he picked up odd jobs — such as crop dusting. Cotton was still a major cash crop in Texas, and hungry fliers could earn a few bucks crisscrossing the fields with spray planes. Enid's cousin Malcolm Lauderdale sometimes assisted Bruce on these jobs, acting as one-man ground crew and all-around gofer. At the crack of dawn, Bruce would take off in a Piper Cub duster and Malcolm would follow in a pickup loaded with poison powder and other supplies. Bruce flew low and slow while Malcolm sped over rural roads trying to keep up. Malcolm then helped Bruce locate a landing site near the field he was dusting.

"We could always find at least a partially suitable place to land on some nearby country road," Malcolm remembered. "There had to be no trees, electric poles, fence posts, or other above-ground obstacles, and the road needed to be wide enough, clear enough with minimal ruts and rocks, and have room to turn around. In some cases, the 'landing strip' met only some of the criteria, but Bruce could always land and take off from anywhere we picked."

The job of loading the poison into the plane fell to Malcolm, since the pilot needed to avoid any possible eye irritation from contact with the nasty stuff.

The cool calm of early morning was the best time for dusting. When everything went just right, Bruce would pass as low as possible over the field and release the fine powder, which would cloud over the plants for a moment and then settle and cling to the dew-damp leaves.

Of course things seldom went perfectly. Each location presented a special set of challenges. Frequently a telephone or electric line ran across one or both ends of the field — or even right across it. These obstacles tended to be home-strung lines that sagged low between distantly spaced poles. Bruce couldn't simply fly over these lines because the insecticide had to be applied very close to the ground. So Malcolm would often use a long pole with a small T-top on it to push the wires up high enough for the airplane to fly underneath.

The procedure worked surprisingly well. Bruce whooshed under the wire, his wingtip slicing only a few feet from the wobbling pole. Malcolm then wiped insecticide off his face and repositioned himself while Bruce turned around and lined up for another pass. One field had a drooping phone line running just above a relatively high fence. As the duster came across the field below the height of the top fence wire, Malcolm lifted the phone line as high as he could. Approaching the fence, Bruce pulled up just enough to slip between the obstacles, then climbed out, turned around, and performed the same maneuver in reverse.

More formidable power transmission lines could not be so casually dealt with, but these were typically strung higher up, and the pilot could fly underneath — so long as he remained mindful of their position. The lines sometimes ran at odd angles with respect to the boundaries of the fields. It was one such situation that spelled the end of the crop-dusting business for Bruce and Malcolm.

They arrived on the job site to find an 880-volt line bisecting a large field. Bruce decided to make his passes parallel to the power line. The grumpy owner complained about the wind conditions,

Crop-duster Bruce with father-in-law and occasional assistant, Eugene MacPherson, 1950.

wondered about the quality of the pilot and equipment, and generally exhibited a negative attitude. Meanwhile Enid had arrived with her two sons and was watching from a parked car nearby.

The owner continued griping to Malcolm while Bruce concentrated on his flying, dodging that high-voltage line as he climbed out to make his turns. To complicate matters, a service line ran off from the main power line at an odd angle near the end of the field. Bruce knew about this too, but near the end of the job, he somehow misjudged the obstacle's position and started his climb-out a little early. A brilliant flash and loud crack immediately told him what had happened. The prop had caught the service line from underneath. The now powerless Cub abruptly nosed down. Bruce managed to pancake into the field, wheels and cowling plowing into the dirt. The tail arced over, and the plane came to a rest upside down.

"It all seemed to be in slow motion," Malcolm remembered. "Enid screamed, the man cursed, and I wondered whether to head for the plane or for the nearest house and try to find a phone to call for help." The man headed for the plane, so Malcolm decided to go for help. Young Bruce Glen, who had been napping, suddenly awoke and asked: "Is my Daddy dead?"

That was the question on everyone's mind. But before Malcolm could turn the truck around, he saw Bruce climb out of the wreck and begin walking around, assessing the damage. Everyone breathed a sigh of relief — except for Bruce, who was angry with himself for his stupid mistake. Physically he was uninjured, but his pride had suffered a severe blow. "I don't crash airplanes very often," he explained years later, still annoyed by his mistake. In fact it would be the only crash of his career due to pilot error.

* * *

Meanwhile, *Trade-a-Plane* had distributed Bruce's Norseman-for-sale ad far and wide. One of the publication's avid readers was prominent Christian missionary William Cameron Townsend, founder of the interdenominational Wycliffe Bible Translators and the Summer Institute of Linguistics (SIL). The Wycliffe organization focused on producing high-quality translations of the Bible in native languages and trying to mitigate the cultural impact of encroaching civilization. SIL helped accomplish these ends through literacy training for native speakers and linguistics training for missionaries. In 1948 Townsend had also founded the Jungle Aviation and Radio Service (JAARS) in Peru as a logistics and technical support arm of SIL. The missionaries relied on airplanes to supply their remote outposts. JAARS operations were now expanding, and Townsend was looking for suitable aircraft.

The Noorduyn Norseman was ideal for his purposes. So William Cameron Townsend contacted Bruce K. Hallock, and in August of 1950 he traveled to Austin to consummate the deal.

The deal was that JAARS would put $4,000 in escrow, payable upon delivery of the Norseman. JAARS would also pay Bruce's expenses associated with transfer of the aircraft to Lima, Peru.

So it came to pass that the sale of the Norseman, that quintessential emblem of bush-piloting romance, actually opened up an opportunity for an incomparable adventure. Bruce and Enid would fly to Lima, Peru. A young SIL missionary from Illinois named Bub Borman would accompany them as copilot. Enid's official role, if anyone were to ask, was radio operator. The two boys, Bruce Glen and Donald, would stay in Austin with their grandparents.

Chapter 8

AWAY WITH THE NORSEMAN

On September 11, 1950, Noorduyn Norseman NC59888 departed Austin, Texas, for the last time. On board were Bruce and Enid Hallock and missionary Bub Borman. They were headed for Lima, Peru, a 4,000-mile journey across varied and treacherous terrain.

Federal regulations required a brief stop in the border town of Brownsville, Texas. After Bruce affixed his signature to the now-routine Declaration of Temporary Sojourn, the form associated with taking an airplane out of the country, the travelers winged south to Veracruz, Mexico, where they spent the first night. Then it was on across the Yucatán's vast jungles and marshlands to Belize City where Enid was introduced to the charms of the isolated little British colony from which her husband had been hauling lobster. She noted that almost everyone wore clean white clothes. Prunes were served as an imported delicacy in this remote land. They spent two days visiting friends and walking around the quaint and exotic town, taking in the smells of the fish market and the amiable King's English. Everything closed at 9 P.M., and people were given to greeting anyone on the streets with a cheerful "Good night."

Bruce filed a flight plan for Panama, and later in the morning than he would have liked, the Norseman took off and continued its southward migration. The travelers soon realized that, in this part of the world, it's best to get your flying done in the morning and be on the ground by the time the afternoon thunderstorms arrive. Maybe the storms appeared a bit early on this particular day, for even as the Norseman crossed the Gulf of Honduras, towering thunderheads loomed on all sides. The travelers only had permission to overfly Honduras — not to land in that country. But the threatening weather gave them no choice. So Bruce headed for the northwestern Honduran city of San Pedro Sula, some 16 miles inland from the gulf.

Since this stop wasn't on the flight plan, fussy military authorities detained the party on general suspicions. A simple phone call to Tegucigalpa, the capital, should have cleared up the matter, but the hapless *norteamericanos* had landed on a national holiday when the country's phone system was totally shut down. So the party was put under "house arrest" in a hotel and told they could go anywhere in town—except to the airport. The detained travelers found entertainment by sitting in the park and watched a large military parade move through the town.

The following day the authorities in Tegucigalpa still couldn't be reached for some reason. Finally the local military commander came by the hotel and, in his broken English, announced, "We decide you good people. Now you go."

So they went. Seven hundred nonstop miles across the mountains and jungles of Honduras, Nicaragua, and Costa Rica brought the wayfarers to the western end of Panama. The city of David, the intended destination for this leg of the trip, was socked in. So the Norseman set down on a grassy strip at Puerto Armuelles, some 30 miles farther west on the Pacific coast. This time no one questioned the unscheduled stopover. Puerto Armuelles was the hub of a United Fruit Company plantation, and the place where Bruce had landed was like a big park, with beautifully kept lawns accented by palm, mango, and teak trees. Enid called it "a ready-made paradise." The travelers were invited into the home of a gracious couple and stayed for two days while waiting for official permission to proceed. During this time, Bruce flew over to David to refuel. Several plantation workers went along for the ride and were impressed enough with the experience to purchase lottery tickets incorporating the Norseman's registration number.

The travelers knew they had to go to Panama City to get permission to continue into Colombia, but they couldn't contact anyone to get clearance to fly into the Canal Zone, a restricted area. Finally Bruce decided to proceed without a flight plan, hoping to negotiate permission by radio en route.

"All the way I expected us to be shot at," wrote Enid. "We couldn't pick up anything on radio. Each minute seemed like an hour." But lucky 59888 landed in one piece. The three travelers spent two days in the Canal Zone and Panama City before obtaining permission to enter Colombia.

Following the isthmus, the Norseman flew east-southeast over Panama's Darién province. The Indians inhabiting this stretch of jungle were said to be so unfriendly that only one stranger had ever returned from their land—and he by feigning insanity. The Norseman's shadow fluttered on across the Serranía del Darién and passed into Colombia. Soon the jungle gave way to the Gulf of Urabá, which forms the crook between Central and South America. Ominous weather persuaded the travelers to land at the little Colombian port town of Turbo.

The airport, which existed primarily as a refueling stop for Pan American Airways, was operated by a couple who lived on the premises. They fed the travelers and advised them against going into town. So the three were put up for the night in a primitive two-story house on the airport. The walls in Bruce and Enid's room were just one board thick. Bugs buzzed around a bare light bulb mounted on a very high ceiling. Outside a diesel generator chugged away, keeping the bulb burning brightly. When it came time to turn in for the night, Bruce and Enid searched for the light switch, which was not to be found, neither inside nor outside the room. They couldn't reach the bulb, and their hosts had gone to bed. Hours passed, and Bruce and Enid lay on the bed staring at their well-lit surroundings. Then sometime after midnight, the door creaked open just a crack.

An arm reached in and gingerly lifted a wire off a nail. The light went out.

* * *

By morning light the Norseman flew south over forests rich in hardwood and rubber trees. Ahead loomed the Colombian Andes, sheer cliff faces converging into jagged snowcapped peaks. Bruce climbed to 13,000 feet. The breathtaking vista stretched on and on.

Then the engine started acting up. The pulse wasn't right. The temperature was rising. And fuel consumption was too high. Suddenly the spectacular vertical terrain lost its appeal. Bruce was glad their load was relatively light. Back in Austin, when planning this trip, they had invited one of Enid's cousins and her husband to come along. The invitation had been earnestly considered and ultimately declined. And given the current situation, that was probably just as well. The extra weight might have proven too much. But as things were, the Norseman sputtered on, holding its altitude and finally setting down at a Colombian Army base near the city of Cali.

The safe landing wasn't the only thing causing Bruce to smile. As he taxied off the runway, he noticed a line of AT-6s. These U.S.-built trainers were powered by the same Pratt & Whitney R-1340 as the Noorduyn Norseman. This fact boded well for the presence of compatible spare parts and savvy mechanics. Surely something could be worked out.

But these gringos in distress would be at the mercy of their guests. Having traveled before in Mexico and Central America, the Hallocks knew about *la mordida* — literally "the bite" — the petty bribery that is part of the customary way of getting things done in this part of the world. Almost any official who did anything for you took a bite out of the cost.

So the travelers were prepared to "negotiate." Instead they were greeted by generous hospitality and eager cooperation. The Colombian Army mechanics swarmed over the Norseman. Expecting the reckoning to come later, the travelers went off to enjoy themselves in town.

In 1950 Cali's notoriety as the home of a ruthless Colombian drug cartel was still far in the future. The beautiful mountain city with sparkling streams rushing under white bridges was marked by unusual and lovely architecture. Formal manners and etiquette were the norm. In the hotel dining room, gentlemen were required to wear coats—even to breakfast.

About this time a newspaper back in Austin reported the trio missing "somewhere over the Andes." They were behind schedule and hadn't been heard from, so some reporter had assumed the worst.

For two full days, the Colombian mechanics worked on the Norseman. They discovered bad bearings in the magneto. They didn't have the necessary replacement parts, but they did have complete new magnetos. In order to keep from disturbing their inventory, they decided to swap the insides of one of their new magnetos for the Norseman's worn parts. (Presumably the defective magneto that now resided in the Colombian inventory was some-

Colombian military mechanics at work on the Norseman. Bruce and Enid standing by.

how marked as such.) They also installed a new ignition harness and tachometer. When the airplane was ready to go, Bruce braced himself for the bill. But the Colombians wouldn't take a cent for all their trouble — not even a little "bite."

But in Ecuador it would be quite a different story. Leaving Cali the revitalized Noorduyn hummed along the western slopes of the Andes. A general south-southwest heading maintained for some 460 miles took the travelers across the equator and finally landed them in Santiago de Guayaquil, Ecuador's largest city. Here the greedy authorities demanded hundreds of dollars in "airport usage fees." This was eventually negotiated down to about $40 — still a hefty sum for the times.

The bustling seaport was situated on the Gulf of Guayaquil, an arm of the Pacific Ocean. In the middle of the night, the travelers' sleep was interrupted by some sort of festive procession passing below their hotel windows.

Continuing south along the Pacific coast, the Norseman encountered a heavy overcast. Bruce stayed low — very low. He skimmed along down close to the waves, below the tops of the trees on shore. Birds scattered to keep out of the way. Enid said she could count the teeth missing in the mouth of a fellow who waved at them. After a couple of hours of sweating it out at this non-altitude, they reached Talara, an oil town on Peru's northern Pacific coast.

Although they had arrived in Peru, they were still nearly 600 miles from Lima, their destination. Peru's arid coastal plain stretched before them as a vast expanse of rock and sand broken only by the occasional oasis or meager river. This band of desert, which ran the length of the country from north to south, was so dry that only a few of the rivers draining the western Andean slopes had sufficient volume to reach the sea before evaporating totally.

As was typical for this time of year, a heavy fog, known locally as *la garúa*, shrouded the coast around Lima. But this endemic murkiness did not dampen the spirits of the three souls winging into

Lima. They were glad to have arrived safely, and happy to turn the Norseman over to its new owners.

* * *

Bruce and Enid spent a week in Lima. Again they were impressed with the formal customs of this part of the world. Suave gentlemen and fur-coated women strolled among the grand hotels, colonial façades, and magnificent churches. All meals were served in courses. In the afternoon high tea could be taken in myriad elegant establishments. "The waiters have a swish and style to their service," wrote Enid, "and one feels that he must respond accordingly." And over this old-world formality hung an air of repression. Signs of the dictatorship abounded — price controls and stern armed guards at every turn.

Bruce and Enid stayed with a missionary family who had a large household in the suburbs. Other missionaries and so-called "contacts" — translators who knew Spanish and the tribal languages — also shared the house.

The missionaries encouraged their guests to visit their base camp on the other side of the Andes. Still feeling adventurous, Bruce and Enid accepted the offer. They wanted to see more of the country, and they soon learned that urbane Lima was a world apart from the rest of Peru.

They traveled by train high into the Andes. The track crossed viaducts spanning black-walled gorges and tunneled through frozen mountains. The train reached 14,800 feet, which made this the highest passenger route in the world at the time. They arrived in Huáncayo, a mountain city known for its weekly fairs, where the inhabitants of the surrounding areas sold food and handicrafts. Bruce and Enid suffered from the mountain sickness. "We could barely lift our heads," wrote Enid, "and all around us those robust Indians were actually running!"

From Huáncayo they traveled by train (a different gauge) to the bleak little mining town of La Oroya. There they transferred to a bus of sorts, actually a converted Ford truck. It was packed with humanity; the cheapest seats were on top of the vehicle. Enid wrote:

> For fourteen hours we sat on one board plank and leaned back against another. We couldn't fall over because there were 22 people in just the front half of the bus. We couldn't count the ones in the back because there were too many dogs, babies, chickens, and sacks of this and that. We made many stops along the way for various reasons. Once, a man was trying to throw his wife off the truck, and she, with reason, objected. A long, hot argument ensued, and we were sorry for the 70th time that we couldn't understand more Spanish.

After a three-hour wait in Cerro de Pasco, located in a constant howling sleet storm at some 14,000 feet, they boarded another bus and started down the eastern slopes of the Andes. These routes through Peru's high plateau were known for their breathtakingly beautiful vistas, but the unpaved roadways themselves were second cousins to riverbeds. In the dark and fog Bruce and Enid couldn't even see the precipices that dropped off practically right under the vehicle's wheels. They could only hear the grinding of the engine and the river roaring through the gorges below. At 2 A.M., they arrived at a lovely tourist hotel in Huánuco. Here they waited a day, because traffic flow on the single-lane road alternated directions each day. More busses and truck-like busses carried them down the mountains. One truck's cab was extended to either side to accommodate five people in front. Suffering from the fumes coming up through the floorboards, Enid insisted that she wanted to get in back. "Oh, no," said the driver. "You can't get in the back. You're first class."

Nearly a week after leaving Lima, the travelers arrived in Pucallpa, situated on the banks of the Ucayali River, one of the main headwaters of the Amazon. Beyond this outpost of civilization, the jungle stretched on and on. The missionary base camp lay only a few miles downriver from Pucallpa. Bruce and Enid spent several days as guests of the missionaries. At night drums throbbed in the distance.

The missionaries of the Summer Institute of Linguistics specialized in gaining the trust of groups that had had no previous sustained contact with outsiders. One of their techniques for initiating relations (heard of, but not witnessed by Bruce and Enid) was to circle a native village with a small plane and lower a basket containing machetes and other useful gifts. Flying in a tight circle supposedly kept the descending basket somewhat stationary over the ground. When the basket reached the ground, the rope was released. It was a tricky business, considering the mistrust and hostility of some of the tribes. There had been killings.

Another technique was to send a couple of women out with a shortwave radio to initiate contact with a group. In theory the natives saw the women as less threatening. Those who made initial contact would treat basic medical needs. They used the radio to call in airdrops of medicine and supplies. So the Jungle Aviation and Radio Service worked hand-in-glove with SIL. JAARS already had several small airplanes at this jungle base, and the larger Norseman would be an important addition to their fleet. In fact the new plane had already arrived at Pucallpa from Lima, and Bruce and Enid watched as it was hoisted up and fitted with floats.

When they were ready to leave, Bruce and Enid opted to take the biweekly flight back to Lima. So a Fawcett Airlines DC-3 carried them high over the tortuous mountain roads that had taken days to traverse. The flight only lasted a couple of hours, but the DC-3 climbed up to 20,000 feet. Passengers had to breathe through oxygen tubes, and women were cautioned to remove their lipstick, as the grease would be a fire hazard if it contacted the oxygen.

Later that night at the Lima airport, Bruce and Enid boarded a Panagra DC-4 bound for Miami, Florida.

Fitting floats onto the Norseman in Pucallpa, Peru. Note new registration on fuselage and painted-over US registration still visible on tail.

* * *

Divested of the Noorduyn Norseman and temporarily sated with adventure, Bruce was eager to get back into aeronautical engineering and continue working on his airplane project. Also, a third child was on the way, and he felt he needed to start earning a reliable income. So for the first time since working at Wright Field before the war, Bruce K. Hallock did what millions of Americans have done — he sent out his résumé.

One of his applications landed at the Chance Vought Corporation in Grand Prairie, Texas, near Dallas. At the time, Chance Vought was working on the still-experimental F7U Cutlass, a tailless jet fighter for the Navy. So it was with particular pleasure that Bruce greeted an offer of employment from the company. In November 1950 the family moved to Grand Prairie, and Bruce went to work as an engineer in the Flight Test Section.

Bruce worked exclusively on the Cutlass program and on only one airplane: Prototype Number 6. He installed and maintained the oscillograph, which recorded all movements of the controls, control surfaces, landing gears, and other moving parts during the test flights. The oscillograph recorded these data on tape for later analysis. A camera also photographed the instrument panel during flight.

The Cutlass was an innovative design and quite advanced for its time. It would eventually become the first production tailless military aircraft, the first Navy aircraft with swept wings, the first production aircraft with afterburning engines, and the first Navy aircraft with a high-pressure hydraulic system. Its tricycle landing gear and pressurized cockpit were still unusual in fighter aircraft of the time. So it was an exciting project.

At home Bruce continued to work on his Road-A-Plane, building wing ribs on a coffee table. Their house in Grand Prairie was situated right under the flight path for the nearby naval air station, and formations of F4U Corsairs regularly thundered overhead.

During this time Bruce took further advantage of the GI Bill and attained his commercial instrument rating at Redbird Airport (now Dallas Executive Airport) in a BT-13. In July 1951, Enid gave birth to a third son, Gary. And later that month, the family let go of their remaining Stinson Voyager, selling it for $1,700.

F7U Cutlass.

Little by little the financial picture improved. And by and by Bruce began to yearn for something more than a punch-card job. He wanted to get back into flying. And the family missed Austin. So after working at Chance Vought for less than a year, Bruce handed in his resignation. His supervisors pleaded with him to reconsider, telling him he was one of their best men and that his deficient knowledge of electronics was well covered by his knowledge of airplanes. They suggested he just take a leave of absence, but Bruce had made up his mind. So on his separation sheet they wrote: "Rehire if possible." But no such possibility would ever arise.

* * *

Back in Austin, Bruce was looking forward to working on his Road-A-Plane, renovating an old house that he and Enid had purchased, and of course engaging in some kind of profitable enterprise.

So normal life resumed—for a few months, at least. Around this time, Bruce got a call from the U.S. Justice Department requesting that he come in and answer a few questions concerning the sale of the Norseman. The Declaration of Temporary Sojourn that he'd so casually signed upon leaving the country with the Norseman had contained a clause requiring that the airplane return within six months. Confident that he could easily clear up any lingering problems by just telling the truth, he cheerfully submitted to a deposition. Nothing more was said until about a week later when, in the wee hours of the morning, he was awakened by pounding at the door. Bleary-eyed Bruce opened the door, and a man immediately stuck his foot in so it couldn't be closed.

The intruder identified himself as a U.S. marshal and asked if he was speaking to Bruce King Hallock.

"Yes."

"You're under arrest. You've got to come with me right now."

"Where am I going?"

"Down to the jailhouse."

Bruce protested that he needed to get dressed. The marshal indulged this whim but would not let his prisoner out of sight, even following him into the bathroom.

Bruce was soon out on bail, but the charge was serious: violation of the Neutrality Act, specifically exporting an implement of war without a permit. Never mind that the implement in question—an old single-engine cargo plane—was sold to missionaries in Peru whose activities and intentions were undeniably peaceful. Bruce had failed to file a "request for consummating a sale out of the country," and in the eyes of the law that little error made him as guilty as any arms smuggler. The indictment was titled: "The United States Government versus Bruce K. Hallock: a Criminal Offense." And to make matters worse, the government had an incriminating sworn deposition from the accused.

With such an airtight case, the prosecutor could not resist the temptation to rack up an easy victory. So Bruce was arraigned before a federal magistrate. The trial was scheduled for Brownsville, Texas, the scene of the "crime," the point of departure for the purported implement of war.

Bruce found a lawyer in Brownsville who was familiar with the jury pool in the area. The federal judge assigned to the trial was none other than former Texas Governor James Allred, and Bruce's savvy lawyer proceeded to select jurors who were known political foes of the judge. Meanwhile Bruce and Enid lined up a slew of character witnesses, which the lawyer used to help show that his client was no treacherous criminal but just an honest guy caught up in a bureaucratic nightmare. Essentially Bruce's defense amounted to an argument that this kind of benign commerce was not what the law was intended to curtail, and his only transgression was a failure to submit the appropriate forms.

The prosecution, on the other hand, had gone to considerable expense to bring in witnesses in support of its case. Among them was an executive of the Summer Institute of Linguistics and the president of the Austin bank that had held the escrow payment for the Norseman while it was being delivered. The testimony of both these witnesses actually bolstered the image of Bruce as an upstanding, law-abiding citizen and mere victim of circumstances.

Nevertheless, on the basis of the facts and the letter of the law, the government had a tight case. And at the end of the day, Judge Allred's instructions to the jury included a twenty-minute lecture to the effect that anybody who had paid attention to the proceedings would decide to convict the defendant. So everyone (except perhaps Bruce's lawyer) was surprised when the jury returned with the verdict: NOT GUILTY.

The celebration was brief. Although cleared of the charges, Bruce was now deep in debt. He had given the lawyer $200 up front and had promised to pay off the balance of the $1,100 fee within a year. Considering his other trial-related expenses and the family's now shaky financial situation, this was a tall order calling for drastic action. So once again the résumés went out.

Chapter 9
FROM EXECUTIVE PILOT TO TEST PILOT

After leaving Chance Vought, Bruce found a series of odd jobs that kept him in the cockpit, including instructing part time at Browning Aerial Service in Austin. Finally, through his ever-widening network of professional contacts, he learned of an opening for an executive pilot in San Antonio.

Bruce now held all the requisite licenses and ratings — so he applied. And in August 1952, he became an employee of the Fair Oil Company, which operated a Twin Beech and a Lockheed Lodestar. Bruce piloted the Beech and copiloted the Lodestar with his boss, Tex Reeves. The company eventually traded the Lodestar for a DC-3.

Bruce's main passenger was company CEO Ralph E. Fair, and the most common destinations were Houston, Brownsville, Laredo, and Midland. When asked where he was going, Bruce was likely to respond: "Fair to Midland."

Fair owned a small Mexican island near Tampico where he maintained a resort home. A landing strip on the island ran from shore to shore—just long enough to bring in the Lodestar. Tex and Bruce would drop off guests at the island and then fly into Tampico to refuel and stay overnight in a hotel.

The job with Fair proved to be a turning point and harbinger of things to come. Bruce liked the work. The pay was decent, and there was enough free time for him to pursue his Road-A-Plane project. The lawyer in Brownsville got paid off, and things were looking pretty good. The only problem was that Bruce and Tex Reeves had incompatible work styles. After about a year, Reeves edged Bruce out of the job and replaced him with a personal friend.

* * *

Leaving Fair Oil Company, Bruce felt confident that he could do just as well or better someplace else. The burgeoning executive aviation market looked promising for someone with his skills and temperament. New postwar designs were coming out, and Bruce had been keeping an eye on the latest developments.

One of the new airplanes that had piqued his interest was the de Havilland 104 Dove. On stopovers in Dallas, Bruce had visited the local distributor and checked out the sleek twin engine. The tricycle landing gear; supercharged, six-cylinder, inverted in-line engines; and the roomy cabin set the British-built Dove apart. It was Britain's first successful postwar civil aircraft. The prototype had flown in September 1945, just as World War II was drawing to a close. The Dove was developed as a feeder airliner for Commonwealth nations but was also marketed worldwide as an executive transport. It was touted as an alternative to the ubiquitous Beech Model 18 (Twin Beech), and Bruce was impressed by the airplane's unusual lines and modern features.

Searching for a new job, Bruce happened to make the acquaintance of business tycoon and bon vivant Bert Beveridge, who had recently purchased a Dove and now needed a pilot. Beveridge was impressed with Bruce, offering him the job upon their initial introduction.

So in December 1953, Bruce became the sole pilot and chief custodian of de Havilland Dove N1588V. This specimen was the new Model 6a with 380-hp Gypsy Queen 70-2 engines and an eight-passenger executive interior. Its original silver and green colors were soon replaced by a softer light-brown and cream scheme. Everywhere it landed, the Dove caught admiring looks.

The first winter on the job, Bruce continued living in and flying out of San Antonio. But by the summer of 1954, the whole Hallock family had packed up and moved to Flint, Michigan, Beveridge's base of operations. The unfinished Road-A-Plane also made the migration, towed on a trailer behind an old Plymouth.

Bert Beveridge had made his millions in the automobile transport business, namely trucking new cars from the factories in Michigan to dealerships throughout the nation. But his passion was polo, and he spent a great deal of time pursuing the high-society sport. There were numerous business trips around the country, but once a week during polo season, Bruce flew Beveridge and his friends to Chicago's Oak Brook Polo Grounds. Two playing fields were situated end to end with an unpaved service drive running between them. On game days, the goal posts were removed so small planes could land using the length of the two 300-yard fields. "It was tight with the Dove," Bruce said, "but I never had any problem." The airplanes parked off to the side, the goal posts were reinstalled, and the games commenced.

* * *

Bert Beveridge had good people looking after the day-to-day operation of his business interests, which allowed him ample time for play. Besides flying to the Chicago polo grounds, Bruce made frequent trips to a ranch in Alabama where the Beveridges raised polo ponies along with cattle. He also began to fly down to Delray Beach, Florida, where Beveridge had leased an entire polo complex. The Beveridges preferred Florida. "Michigan is no place to live," Bert told Bruce. "It's just a place to make money."

B. K. Hallock, pilot and guardian of de Havilland Dove N1588V.

Bruce continued flying for Bert Beveridge for six years. During that time, the Hallock family moved to Florida to live in a house on the polo grounds in Delray Beach for a few months. After that they moved briefly to Alabama and lived on the Beveridge ranch. Then it was back to Michigan for a few more years. And the family grew. Number-four son, Mark Stephen, arrived in December 1955.

Bruce liked flying the Dove, and the pay was excellent. He did everything, from scheduling maintenance to vacuuming out the interior. Most of the flying was pretty routine, but there were interesting moments. One Sunday evening after the polo games in Chicago, Beveridge wanted to fly down to his Alabama ranch. It was a night flight, and they arrived over their destination quite late. Since the ranch's landing strip was unlighted, Bruce headed for nearby Selma. Unfortunately, the uncontrolled Selma airport had already turned off its lights. From high above, Bruce could see the airport all right by the glow of the nearly full moon. But he knew that once he got down low and had to view the runway horizontally, visibility would not be good. So he and Beveridge deliberated. Bruce had had some experience landing without lights back in Austin at St. Edward's Airport, and he told his employer he was willing to take one pass at it. "If it doesn't seem feasible, we'll have to go over to Montgomery. And if we try it and hit a deer or a cow or something, why we're out of the airplane business."

Beveridge agreed to take a chance, and the Dove descended toward the darkened airport. Bruce chose his landing direction by the position of the moon, keeping it behind him to avoid being dazzled. During the approach, he kept the landing lights off because they too could cause a disorienting glare. The landing gear thumped down and locked. The flaps went down. Bruce waited until he was right over the runway to flip on the landing lights. The touchdown was as smooth and anticlimactic as any he had ever made under the most ideal conditions.

Bruce's passengers were typically Beveridge's business associates or his friends and family. One of the more notable individuals to board the Dove was labor leader Jimmy Hoffa. Being an executive in the trucking and automobile business, Beveridge must have had an ambivalent relationship with the Teamsters Union big shot. On the face of it, they were natural adversaries, but it later became known that the two men had conspired in some crooked business deals. Bruce explained it simply by saying: "It's good to be friends with your enemies."

Anyway, Jimmy Hoffa happened to be in Rochester, New York, and needed to get to Detroit in a hurry. For whatever reason, Beveridge had a vested interest in getting Hoffa to his destination that day, so he asked Bruce to fetch him.

Rain was falling in Rochester when Bruce landed. He opened the door, and Hoffa and a couple of his cronies splashed out to the waiting airplane and climbed aboard. The Dove had so-called "club seating," meaning the passenger seats faced each other, with small tables that could be folded out from the wall in between. Hoffa plopped down and flung his feet up on the opposite seat — muddy, wet shoes and all. Bruce said nothing but later confided: "I immediately didn't like him." The flight to Detroit went without further incident, but afterwards Bruce had to clean up the mess.

And then there was the midair collision. Bruce was flying the Dove alone at night. He was about 9,000 feet over Austin, Texas, headed for San Antonio. The air was calm, and the flying was smooth. Then — wham! "I jumped out of my seat," he said later. "It felt like the wing had come off." But a quick check revealed no problem. Everything seemed to be intact and functional. Bruce had no idea what had happened. So he began a slow, cautious descent. Upon landing in San Antonio, he got out a flashlight and looked around. On the left side of the nose was a smear of blood and guts, the remains of a high-flying duck or goose.

Despite the occasional mess inside or outside the airplane, the job's pace was pretty easygoing. Beveridge allowed Bruce to bring family members along on trips and occasionally make detours to take care of personal business. Bruce preferred to have the Dove serviced at Dallas Aero, and one such occasion provided the justification for a visit to Austin. The whole family—Enid and four boys—came along for the ride. On the way, bad weather forced Bruce to fly high—all the way up to 16,000 feet, as he recalled. The Dove was not pressurized and not equipped with oxygen. "Everybody fell asleep," Bruce said, "except me." But this author also remembers the trip and attests that he also stayed awake.

* * *

When not flying or caring for the Dove, Bruce was free to work on his tailless project. Beveridge had a large hangar at Flint's Bishop Airport to house the Dove, and he allowed Bruce to work on his airplane there. The swept wings took shape, and the fabric covering went on—grade-A linen, doped and rib stitched. Enid helped sew the envelopes and did some of the stitching. The airplane received a blue-and-yellow paint scheme, with the registration number appearing on the outside of each vertical fin: N2721C.

And at some point the name on the nose changed—the Road-A-Plane became the Road Wing. When asked about the change, Bruce said he wanted a classier name. "Road-A-Plane just sounded like some kind of cheap game," he said.

In preparing the Road Wing for flight tests, Bruce examined every facet of the airframe, pondering all conceivable problems. For some time he had realized that the center of gravity was too far aft. He corrected this by adding weight. Fifty pounds in the form of lead-filled frozen orange juice cans (made of steel in those days) went into a box fixed to the floor forward of the copilot's seat (there were no rudder pedals on the right side).

Another worry concerned the main landing gear. It was well secured to the keel, but Bruce began to worry that the lateral support might not be adequate under extraordinary conditions, such as a blowout or if he hit something on the runway. So as a last-minute precaution, he attached cables from the base of the nose gear back to the lower extremity of each main landing gear near the axle. This would restrain them from bending or breaking backwards in the event of a mishap.

And considering the prospect of a mishap while aloft, Bruce worried that the air pressure against the cabin door would impede a swift bailout. So he replaced the door-hinge pins on the pilot's side with a wire that ran up under the window and terminated in a loop that he could easily pull to pop off the door. "I was ready to use it," he later declared.

Finally on a gray November day in 1957, Bruce moved the Dove out of the way, and the Road Wing emerged from the hangar ready to roll down the runway. He first planned a series of high-speed taxi tests to get a feel for how the controls would respond and to make sure the rest of the airframe was ready for actual flight. Even

Road Wing ready for maiden flight. Note wing slots.

though he didn't intend to fly that day, Bruce was prepared for anything. So on went the military flight helmet and parachute. His friend Stu Ellston stood by with buckets of sand and a fire extinguisher.

Obtaining clearance from the tower, Bruce taxied out and lined up at the end of the runway. He built up speed gradually. Everything went okay — except when he eased back on the wheel. The plane showed no inclination to rotate on its main gear. Maybe he hadn't been moving fast enough. So he tried another run.

Traveling faster this time, Bruce still could not achieve enough elevator authority to raise the nose. The air speed reached 90 mph as the Road Wing neared the runway's end. Bruce later admitted that not being able to get the nose up on those initial high-speed runs was probably a lucky thing. "If I had," he said, "I would have been in trouble." "Trouble" meaning the plane might have lifted off and stalled.

But he would eventually have to raise the nose in order to take off. Back at the hangar, Bruce brooded on the matter for a while. Lack of elevator authority is an issue common to tailless airplanes,

Road Wing and her proud creator-test pilot.

as the elevons near the trailing-edge tips of the swept wings are not very far aft of the center of gravity. On a conventional design, the relatively longer moment of the fuselage, combined with the prop wash blowing over the empennage, provides adequate leverage for low-speed pitch control. Tailless designs require other strategies to help lever the nose wheel off the ground on takeoff. Bruce finally decided that a higher angle of attack would solve the problem. The Road Wing needed to sit on its landing gears with the nose aimed just a little higher.

As an experiment, he wrapped a piece of coat-hanger wire around the scissor spring on the nose wheel strut to prevent it from compressing. This tilted the nose up by just a couple of degrees. Bruce wanted to proceed incrementally. So expecting more of the same, he returned to the runway and applied full power.

"It just leaped into the air!" he said. "It surprised me!"

That first unplanned flight on December 1, 1957, was only a short hop. Bruce landed immediately after leaving the ground. Then he did it again — and again. He made about five of these straight-along-the-runway flights to make sure he had enough elevator authority to fly safely. He also gently tested the aileron control on these flights. Eventually he traded the coat hanger for a couple of stout springs.

The next step was to make a turn. Bishop Airport had two major runways intersecting at approximately 90 degrees. Bruce obtained permission from the control tower to take off from one, make a shallow left turn, and immediately land on the other. He executed the maneuver with no problem, which encouraged him to venture further. For the next flight, he left the runway behind and circled the field.

After a few months of these test hops, Bruce decided he was ready for the first "official" flight. All these little test flights had been off the record and never were noted in the Road Wing's logbook. The Federal Aviation Administration had not yet granted permission for the airplane to fly. They hadn't inspected it or done the final paperwork. So at his leisure, Bruce called the FAA and informed them he was ready to fly his experimental airplane. On October 23, 1958, several officials arrived at the hangar on the corner of Bishop Airport. In the 1950s, airplanes built by individuals were not as common as they would later become with the rise in popularity of homebuilts. The Road Wing was a real novelty. The bemused federal officials conducted their inspection, signed the paperwork, and stayed to observe the "first" flight.

Enid drove with three of the boys in the family's VW Microbus to a vantage point at the end of the runway on the other side of airport where they could watch the Road Wing come over after takeoff. They waited as Bruce double-checked everything. Other light planes took off. The younger boys began playing in the dirt and climbing on the fence. Enid squinted nervously toward the far end of the airport. Then suddenly she yelled, "Here he comes!"

The blue-and-yellow Road Wing sped down the runway toward the waiting family. Then it was in the air. Enid's hands flew to her open mouth. Her breath stopped. Baby Mark stuttered, "Da-da." Six-year-old Gary waved wildly with both hands. Nine-year-old Don became upset with Gary, afraid the waving might distract their father at the controls. The Road Wing yowled overhead, and all heads turned to follow it.

Don later described his feelings: "I remembered being filled with emotion, pride, awe, and even a little reverence at what my dad had accomplished. Somehow I knew what it had taken to make this flight happen."

Bruce flew to a designated test area several miles from the airport. There he performed a series of turns, stalls, and slow-flight maneuvers to ascertain the flight characteristics of his new design. People would later want to know what it was like to fly the Road Wing. How did it fly? "It flies just like an airplane," Bruce would answer, "very much like a Cessna or Stinson." His matter-of-fact tone seemed to imply that, although the design was unconventional, its perfectly normal performance should be no great surprise. When pressed on the matter, Bruce would admit that the Road Wing stalled at a pretty high angle of attack. "So when I landed, the nose was way up," he said. "But this is typical of swept-wing aircraft." For the tests flights, he actually made his landing approaches at a relatively high speed in order to maintain good control.

That first official flight lasted 15 minutes. Bruce taxied back to the hangar where a small group of onlookers and well-wishers had gathered. Although there was no champagne, a sense of occasion surrounded the event. Even the children understood that this moment represented the culmination of years of dreaming, designing, and building. The Road Wing had become a family icon, conceived in the same year as Enid and Bruce's firstborn. The unfinished project had followed the family from Austin to San Antonio and then to Flint, Michigan. Now it had flown—proven itself. Anything seemed possible.

B. K. Hallock in HT-1 Road Wing high over Flint, Michigan, 1958.

For future flight tests, the feds assigned Bruce a restricted area. "I couldn't fly over the city," he remembered. "And I couldn't fly more than 50 miles from the airport—or something like that—for the first 10 hours of flight."

The Road Wing would make just two more flights. The second flight was terminated early when a screw worked loose from the cowling and hit the prop. Bruce said his heart just about stopped when he heard the loud crack. Not knowing the cause of the ominous sound, he landed immediately and found a knick in one propeller blade's leading edge.

The Road Wing's final flight lasted almost an hour. A Piper Tri-Pacer carrying a news cameraman accompanied it aloft. The resulting 16-mm movie footage contains many superb in-flight shots of the Road Wing soaring over the Michigan countryside.

* * *

Certain details of the Road Wing's roadability remained unresolved. Bruce had devised a wheeled jack that allowed one person to detach and fold the wings one at a time. First a caster wheel was attached near the leading-edge tip. Then a pin that held the main spar to the fuselage was removed. With the jack supporting the outer wing, the leading edge was rotated downward by means of a

Road Wing transitioning to road-vehicle mode.

universal joint attached to the rear spar. The strut stayed in place. Then the whole wing was pivoted back until its span was parallel with the fuselage. The top portion of the vertical fin and rudder was folded in flat against the wings and secured.

Since the propeller was to provide propulsion on the roadway, it had to spin within the space between the folded wings. The only problem was that the clearance on this experimental prototype was not sufficient for the two-blade Sensenich. This was not an oversight, as future versions of the Road Wing could have been outfitted with a three- or four-blade propeller of lesser diameter. Meanwhile

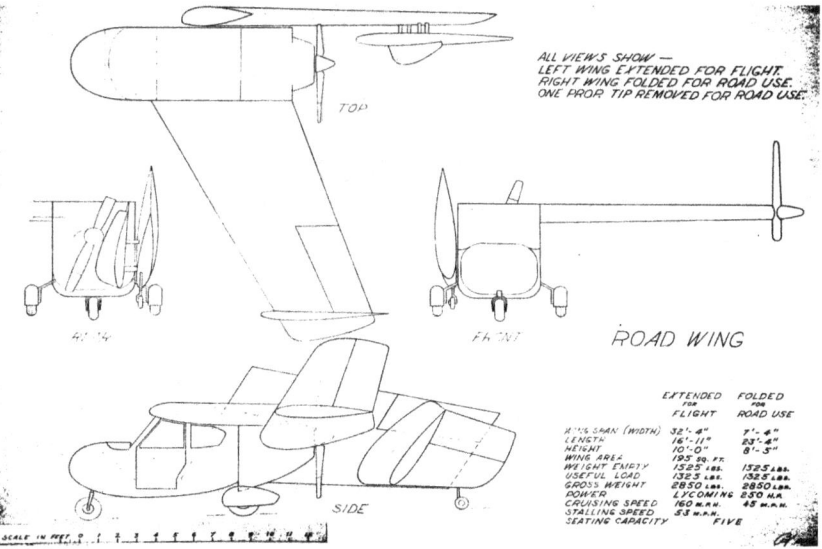

Tentative specifications for Road Wing production model as compared to the existing experimental prototype.

Proposed future development of the Road Wing. Note redesigned rudder, more streamlined body, and removable propeller tips.

Bruce had devised an interim solution for this first experimental model. After completing the flight tests, Bruce cut approximately nine inches off the blade ends. The shortened propeller would work well enough for road use, but the tips would have to be replaced for flight. So he fabricated metal flanges that allowed him to reattach the blade tips. But the Road Wing was never flown after this.

Bruce did some design work on a second version of the airplane, but after completing the flight tests, his interests began to move on. Other more modern aeronautical engineering projects seized his imagination. The Road Wing's day had passed. The unique airplane eventually went into long-term storage in Austin, Texas, where it gathered the dust of the decades.

Oddly, the passage of half a century has not brought the dream of aircraft roadability any closer to everyday reality. On the contrary, the flying car has become a relic of yesterday's future, a quaint notion. Automotive and aeronautical design have diverged in more ways than they have converged. Modern automotive engineering and safety requirements (airbags, crashworthiness, lights, stability, brakes, etc.) seem to have rendered the two vehicle types less compatible than ever. Today's few proponents of roadable airplanes are largely regarded as eccentrics.

With benefit of hindsight, it might be argued that the Road Wing would have stood a better chance of commercial success without the roadability feature. Introducing a tailless airplane to the convention-bound private-plane market was challenge enough without the added novelty of roadability. But it must be remembered that, at the time of the plane's inception, roadability appeared to be a probable, if not inevitable, part of civil aviation's future. Bruce K. Hallock dreamed of that future, and the fact that his vision did not come to pass does not detract from its brilliance. The Road Wing was built as a proof-of-concept, not as a final product. In that regard it was a success, even though the concept never entered the mainstream.

Hallock family and related vehicles, December 1958.

* * *

Soon after the Road Wing's last flight, another major project long in the planning was launched. Bruce and Enid's 1950 trip through Peru had not cured their adventure-travel itch—instead it had only intensified it. Even as they had lumbered over the Andes aboard those crowded bus-trucks, they had daydreamed of more such trips. They had continued to study the region, reading books on Latin America and attending travel lectures. Enid had learned Spanish. Eventually they conceived the idea of driving down the Pan-American Highway all the way to Panama. They would take their time and follow no set schedule. They would take all four boys. The trip became the next focal point of the family's future.

The time seemed right. The Road Wing had flown. Money had been saved. And the boys were of a manageable age (if ever they would be). So in the fall of 1959, with 2,900 cumulative hours in the Dove's cockpit, Bruce resigned from his job as Bert Beveridge's pilot. The family said goodbye to their Michigan friends and headed for Austin, Texas, where they prepared for the grand adventure through Mexico and Central America and on into South America.

It was a remarkable journey. To undertake such a trip alone would have been unusual and daring in its own right. But doing it with his wife and four boys demonstrated extraordinary self-confidence — or foolhardiness — or both. Whatever the motivation, the expedition demonstrated that Bruce K. Hallock's willingness to take on big projects was not limited to aviation.

The trip, which took a full six months, had nothing to do with aviation. It was an interlude in Bruce's career. The journey fulfilled a different need, one related to family and a continuing yearning to experience more of the world. For the boys it was a once-in-a-lifetime adventure. And although they may not have been mature enough to appreciate it, the experience would play a significant role in forming their worldviews.

They traveled through every country in Central America. Bruce had customized the VW Microbus's interior so that all six family members could sleep and eat in it. Most of the time they camped out and cooked on a compact gas stove. It was the eve of the great social and political upheavals that would engulf the region for

The Hallock family and their VW rafting across a river in Costa Rica, 1960.

decades to come. But the traveling Hallocks encountered few problems, and were generally greeted warmly everywhere they went. The roads were still primitive in many places. Between Costa Rica and Panama, they forded dozens of rivers and streams. A log raft carried them across one.

The Darién Gap between Panama and Colombia remained impassable (as it does to this day). So the family left the Microbus in the Canal Zone and flew to Colombia where they spent about a month exploring Medellín and traveling by steamboat on the Magdalena River. Eventually the VW was put aboard a cargo plane and flown to Miami. The family followed by airliner.

* * *

A tragic footnote to the story of de Havilland Dove N1588V: After Bruce left the employ of Bert Beveridge, the airplane was sold to TAG Airlines and converted for use as a commuter air taxi. The registration was changed to N2300H. On January 28, 1970, it departed Burke Lakefront Airport in Cleveland, Ohio, as Flight 730 bound for Detroit, Michigan. About 10 minutes into the flight, the Dove suddenly plunged from the sky and crashed through the ice of Lake Erie, killing all on board—seven passengers and two pilots. After examining the wreckage, the National Transportation Safety Board concluded that the probable cause of the accident was "the in-flight failure of the lower, right, main wing-to-fuselage root joint attach fitting resulting from undetected fatigue cracks in the wing portion of the fitting." In other words, the wing had broken off. These fittings were known to be susceptible to fatigue, and the NTSB's accident report prompted the FAA to require more frequent inspections and replacement of the parts in question.

Chapter 10

POLITICIANS AND RICKSHAWS

The Hallocks returned from their Latin American sojourn in the summer of 1960, the last full year of Dwight Eisenhower's presidency. Democrats hankered to retake the White House, and several prominent leaders were jockeying for the party nomination. One of them was Senator Lyndon Baines Johnson of Texas. As the campaigning geared up and Johnson's travel schedule became more intense, his chief pilot, Harold Teague, started looking for a backup.

Meanwhile Bruce K. Hallock had found plenty of work flying other people's business aircraft out of Austin. At one point, Bruce said, he was in charge of five Twin Beeches. So he was pretty well known around the Austin airport, and his name appeared high on Teague's list of prospects. Eventually Bruce accepted an offer of

Bruce with one of the many Twin Beeches he piloted during the 1960s.

employment from Teague and was suddenly thrust into the tumult of presidential campaigning.

Lyndon Johnson used his Central Texas ranch as a base of operations. The ranch, about 40 straight-line miles west of Austin, had a paved and lighted landing strip. When Bruce started working for him, LBJ had three airplanes—a Beechcraft Bonanza, a Twin Beech (which the Johnsons had dubbed *Redbird*), and a Lockheed Lodestar. Most of the flying was done between the ranch and Austin or other Texas destinations. For longer trips Johnson generally used the airlines. But when LBJ was at the ranch, a constant stream of visitors had to be ferried to and fro.

It was a heady, hectic time. Bruce tried to ignore the deal-making that went on all around him, but he knew some of it was shady. He received his pay in the form of envelopes stuffed with hundred-dollar bills.

And after John F. Kennedy won the Democratic presidential nomination and selected Johnson as his running mate, the pace picked up even more. The ranch received all sorts of high-level visitors, including Kennedy himself. Harold Teague and Bruce flew JFK and his entourage out to the ranch and back in the Lodestar. Bruce did a lot of standing by, just in case Johnson needed the plane for something. Bruce remembered a dinner at the ranch where he sat at the same table with John Connally (then governor of Texas and soon to become secretary of the Navy), Walter Cronkite, Bill Moyers, Sally Quinn, and other notables.

On another occasion Ex-President Harry S. Truman visited the ranch with Kennedy. When the meeting broke up, Teague took Kennedy back to Austin to catch his plane, but Truman wanted to go down to Uvalde, Texas, to visit his old friend John Nance Garner. Garner had been vice president during Franklin Roosevelt's first two terms. Bruce flew Truman in the Twin Beech and actually accompanied Truman on his visit to Garner's house (which Bruce described as "kind of ramshackle"). The spunky politician who had famously disparaged the vice presidency as "not worth a bucket of warm piss" (erroneously reported in prudish newspapers as "a bucket of warm spit") was now confined to a wheelchair. But active Democrats continued to consult Garner throughout his retirement, and he was especially close to Harry Truman.

* * *

Johnson never questioned Bruce's politics. In fact he told Bruce outright that his political leanings didn't matter—he just wanted a good professional pilot. And it was probably just as well that nothing more was said on the subject. Bruce's political background was mixed. He'd come from a long line of Yankee Republicans, but he'd married into a nest of Roosevelt Democrats. In truth he cared little for politics and tended to discuss the subject even less—the perfect attitude for a politician's pilot. Bruce viewed Johnson's profession with a jaundiced eye, while LBJ trusted Bruce implicitly. So they got along fine.

As the campaign heated up, Johnson added another airplane to his fleet—a Convair 240. The 240 was a large postwar twin that had been built for the airlines as a successor to their aging DC-3s. By 1960 these sturdy Convairs were being retired from the airlines, and several of the planes had entered service as executive transports. Harold Teague captained Johnson's Convair. Sometimes Bruce was copilot, but usually he piloted the smaller planes while someone else flew with Teague.

By this time, Johnson was doing much of his flying with American Airlines. As one of the Democrats' corporate supporters, the airline put a plane and crew at Johnson's disposal, and he took full advantage of this generosity. But Johnson still needed his fleet of smaller planes for flying to and from the ranch and getting in and out of other small airfields.

And for Bruce, the job occasionally involved other little chores.

Lyndon Johnson's trademark was his silver Stetson Open Road cowboy hat. He was never without it. And anyone of consequence who visited his ranch received one as a gift. So Johnson's aides bought the hats by the truckload—in all sizes. A whole room at the ranch was given over to shelves full of these hats awaiting bestowal.

One time when Johnson was campaigning out of state, Bruce got a call from one of his aides. Someone had sat or stepped on the senator's hat and crushed it. Johnson wanted Bruce to fly out to the ranch, pick up a new hat, and then meet him with it in Dallas as he came through on his way to somewhere else.

So Bruce (along with Enid and a friend who just went along for the ride) took the Bonanza out to the ranch, picked up the proper size Stetson, and headed for Dallas. The delivery went as planned. Johnson was traveling on an American Airlines plane. The airliner taxied over to the parked Bonanza, and the boarding stairs rolled into place. Bruce walked up and handed over the precious article. Then Johnson was on his way again, prepared to flaunt his iconic headgear at the next campaign stop.

Bruce did not mind playing the role of valet from time to time. He had occasionally performed the same kinds of humble errands for Bert Beveridge. He was aware that his high-flying employers tended to consider an executive pilot little more than a glorified chauffeur. He accepted this state of affairs with cheerful equanimity and an unshakable confidence that his own worth was measured by greater things. The job did not define him; rather he defined the job. And Bruce's ability to avoid even a hint of servility or resentment probably raised his esteem in the eyes of those he served.

Late one night Johnson returned from an out-of-state trip. Bruce met him at Austin's Robert Mueller Municipal Airport with the Twin Beech, ready to fly him home.

"How's the weather, Bruce?" Johnson said as he stepped off the larger plane and started walking toward the Beechcraft.

"Well, it's foggy," Bruce said as he matched Johnson's stride. "It's been foggy a lot of places around here."

"Well, it's up to you," Johnson said, pausing to give Bruce a searching look. "Can we make it or not?"

After another heartbeat, Bruce replied, "Yes, I think we can if we go right away."

"Let's go, then," Johnson said without further hesitation.

And they went. Such is the trust anyone would want to be able to place in his private pilot.

LBJ's Open Road Stetson.

* * *

LBJ surrounded himself with people he could depend on, his wife being foremost among them. Her given name was Claudia Alta, but since childhood everyone had called her Lady Bird. Lyndon usually just called her Bird. And he relied on her utterly. When he climbed back into the airplane after making a campaign speech in the broiling sun, she was right there with a fresh shirt. He'd change as Bruce flew to the next "whistle-stop."

Lady Bird acted as a kind of super social secretary. "She knew all the people wherever they went," said Bruce. "And when we landed somewhere, she would tell LBJ, 'Now the mayor will meet us at the airplane. And the mayor's wife's name is Susie. And they have a little girl 6 years old.' Then LBJ would get out of the airplane and say, 'Hi, Susie, how are you? How's your daughter?' That kind of thing."

So Bruce got an insider's glimpse of the way Johnson operated, and one thing he admired about the man was his ability to catnap. "He'd get into the airplane, sit down, put his head back, and immediately go to sleep," Bruce said with a touch of envy. For someone committed to a frenzied campaign schedule, the ability to fall asleep at the drop of a hat was invaluable.

Everyone stayed busy. Even when he was campaigning out of state, Johnson sometimes called on Bruce. On one occasion LBJ was in St. Louis, Missouri, and needed to get to a campaign event in a little town just south of there. (Bruce couldn't remember the name of the town.) Since the town's airport was too small for the big American Airlines plane in which Johnson and his entourage were traveling, Bruce flew *Redbird* up to St. Louis and picked them up. Somehow making this appearance was important to Johnson.

A heavy rain had fallen the day before, but on this day the weather was clear and quite windy. When the bright-red Twin Beech appeared over the town, the high school band lined up, all smart uniforms and gleaming instruments. The mayor and other townspeople stood ready to greet the next vice president of the United States. And under a big tent, caterers kept the barbecue simmering.

Approaching the airport, Bruce assessed conditions. The wind was at 25 knots with gusts to 35. And it was blowing directly across the airport's sole runway, which was paved but short. "Too short, really," he admitted later. Furthermore, the plane was full. Considering the load and the crosswind, Bruce flew the final approach faster than usual—so he'd have "some reserve control," as he put it. He set the tires on the pavement right at the end of the runway, but he was still rolling at upwards of 90 miles per hour. Braking as best he could while fighting the crosswind gusts, Bruce soon realized he was running out of runway. No matter, he thought, there was some extra space—the grassy overrun area between the end of the runway and the fence.

The tires thumped off the edge of the pavement—and into the soggy Missouri sod. With a sinking feeling, Bruce understood the situation at once. He gunned the engines. "I was in the mud," he said. "And I knew that if I stopped the airplane, I'd never get it moving again. I had to keep going."

With much sloshing and splattering, he managed to get the

Beech back on the pavement. Chagrinned, Bruce taxied *Redbird* over to the waiting crowd, tracking mud all the way. The band struck up a rousing fanfare. The door swung open, and Johnson appeared waving his Stetson, which the wind nearly snatched away. Cheering erupted. Hands were shaken, babies were kissed, and speeches were made.

Then everyone sat down for some barbecue — everyone but Bruce. "I spent the whole time cleaning off the airplane," he said. "The landing gears and wheel wells were caked with mud." Then he added, "I didn't get any barbecue."

* * *

The description "larger than life" seemed to fit Lyndon Johnson perfectly. The man was big and tall—six feet, three inches—and he had a booming voice. "When he talked to you," Bruce said, "he'd put his face right up within 12 inches of your face. You knew you were being talked to. And you felt the only thing to say was, 'Yes, sir, Mr. Senator.' But I never had any problems with him at all." It was a claim that few of LBJ's friends or enemies could make, but Bruce said it with a straight face: "I never had any problems with him at all." Not even the time he turned the tables and actually reproved the big man himself.

An American Airlines Lockheed Electra had landed at Austin's Robert Mueller Municipal Airport to pick up LBJ and whisk him off to some distant engagement. Unfortunately the senator had not yet arrived at the airport. So the crew shut down three of the plane's four engines and waited. The number-four engine had to keep running because it was equipped with a compressor used to start the other three engines. At the time, Austin lacked the special equipment required to start the Electra's turboprop engines if all four were shut down. So it was necessary to keep that one engine running—which was okay for a while, but it was using up fuel. And the airplane could not be refueled when an engine was running. So if the onboard fuel supply dropped below a certain level, the crew would have no choice but to stop the number-four engine and refuel. Then to get the engines restarted, a compressor would have to be brought up from San Antonio, some 80 miles away.

Meanwhile out at the ranch, Bruce was waiting with *Redbird* ready to fly Johnson and his traveling companions in to Austin to meet the Electra. But some last-minute business had detained the senator. As he waited, Bruce monitored the weather reports. Rain was moving through Austin, scattered thunderstorms.

Finally Johnson came striding out and jumped in the airplane, and they took off. Even though the trip normally took less than 30 minutes, Bruce filed an instrument flight plan on account of the "iffy" weather. Once he arrived over Austin, he was put into a holding pattern. The weather was delaying operations, and *Redbird* was about number four in line to land.

By this time the Electra had been sitting on the ground burning fuel for over an hour. The crew was nervously watching their gauges, and Johnson, who was aware of the situation, was also anxious. But the air-traffic controllers were not giving special consideration to VIPs. Inbound flights were landing in the order in which they'd called in.

Alone in the cockpit, Bruce had his hands full dealing with the weather and the air-traffic situation. He hadn't updated his passengers on the situation. The minutes ticked by. Soon he felt a tap on his shoulder and Johnson's hot breath on his cheek. "Bruce, what's the matter here? Why aren't we landing?"

Rain was beating on the windshield, and the airplane was bouncing around, and just then the control tower started issuing instructions.

Bruce raised a commanding hand. "Quiet!" he said and gave the radio his full attention. Then he turned to Johnson. "I'm too busy to talk to you now," he said. "Go sit down and fasten your seatbelt."

Without further protest, Johnson did as he was told. Bruce entered a turn, perhaps exaggerating the bank for dramatic effect.

Redbird eventually landed okay, and Johnson got on the Electra in time to fly on without further complications. Everything turned out fine, and Bruce K. Hallock came away from the episode holding the distinction of being one of the few people (if not the only one) to ever get away with ordering Lyndon B. Johnson to shut up and sit down.

* * *

After the election Bruce quit working for Johnson. Harold Teague continued as chief pilot, but soon after the inauguration he met with tragedy. In mid February 1961, he and copilot Charles Williams were ferrying the otherwise empty Convair 240 to the ranch. Visibility was bad, and somehow they slammed into a hillside. Neither man survived the crash.

Johnson had hinted to both Harold and Bruce that, if he and Kennedy won the election, there would be a job for them both flying Air Force Two, the airplane in which the vice president normally traveled. It would have meant a special commission in the U.S. Air Force and would be a great honor. It was a flattering offer, but neither man took him up on it. Bruce told Johnson he didn't want to move to Washington—which was true—but he was also growing weary of politicians. "Anything those guys ever said had some kind of ulterior motive behind it," Bruce said of the breed in general. "What they said wasn't really what they meant at all."

But it wouldn't be his last encounter with that particular subspecies. Politicians needed pilots, and pilots needed work. So again at various times during the 1960s and '70s, Bruce endured the frantic schedules, the disingenuous utterances, and the cash-filled envelopes. One of his more notable regular passengers was the flamboyant Bob Bullock, who variously served as state representative, assistant attorney general of Texas, Texas secretary of state, comptroller, and eventually lieutenant governor.

And before that, in the early 1960s, Bruce served for a while as chief pilot for the Texas General Land Office. The state owned vast tracts of land for which the records were scant. The land commissioner at the time, Jerry Sadler, wanted to verify the status and uses of the property. In those pre-spy-satellite days, the best way to gather this information was through aerial photography. Sadler asked Bruce to recommend a suitable airplane, and not surprisingly the de Havilland Dove topped the list of possibilities.

Bruce soon found a used Dove for sale, and he and Sadler went to look it over. The land commissioner seemed to be happy with the airplane, satisfied that it was appropriate for the job and reasonably priced. At this point Bruce thought it sensible to point out that, in addition to the practical features, the Dove possessed a particularly pleasing outline and tended to be a real eye-catcher.

This was the wrong thing to say to a state official concerned with the possible appearance of misuse of funds. Sadler gruffly informed Bruce that he didn't give a damn what the plane looked like, he was only concerned with what it could do for the money. So Bruce canned the aesthetic pitch and went back to discussing the Dove's fitness for the task at hand. Eventually Sadler was convinced, and the Land Office purchased the de Havilland Dove — despite its charms.

Sadler also hired a veteran World War II aircraft cameraman, and he and Bruce mounted a large camera in the airplane's floor so pictures could be taken straight down. When the plane was ready, Bruce, copilot Monroe Quillin, and the cameraman began flying grids. They did a lot of work in north Texas and around the Sabine River near Beaumont. They spent days and weeks at a time flying back and forth on precise headings.

Back at the Land Office, they developed the pictures and pieced them together to create big aerial maps of various sections of the state. "The pictures were very good," Bruce said. "I was impressed."

When he wasn't flying or working on the airplane, Bruce was at the Land Office checking maps. At the time, veterans could buy land from the state through a special program. Bruce spent some time verifying the location and acreage of the parcels they'd mapped out. Some of the old deeds dated back to Spanish colonial times. He told of one that described a boundary in terms of the distance a man could walk while smoking one cigarette. To verify the boundary, the Land Office had researched the type of tobacco and rolling paper used during that era. Then they actually produced some authentic period cigarettes and had someone walk in the specified direction while smoking. Later the original boundary markers were discovered remarkably close to where the latter-day ambling smoker had determined they should be.

It was interesting work, but the pay was paltry — under $500 a month — less than half what he had been making flying for Bert Beveridge in Michigan. Jerry Sadler had talked up the job, exaggerating the opportunities and prospects, and Bruce soon realized he could do better elsewhere.

* * *

All the time he was flying politicians and executives, Bruce was yearning to get back to his true passion, engineering. And a job he took in the early 1960s proved to be the impetus he needed. It was truly a transitional job, involving equal parts flying and engineering.

Bill Bales was a high roller, a promoter, and a bit of a shyster with a talent for harnessing other people's money. He had set up an operation in Austin to manufacture golf carts. He needed someone to organize and set up his production line and troubleshoot the customers' technical problems. He also needed a pilot for his Twin Beech. He needed a man like Bruce K. Hallock.

Bales put Bruce in charge of the factory, including about 30 employees. The golf carts sold all over the country. Orders rolled in; business was good. Custom-built trailers carried off up to three dozen of the little vehicles at a time. When customers had trouble with their golf carts or needed parts in a hurry, Bruce would fly out. He knew all about the carts — how they were put together, their problems and quirks.

He earned better money than he had at the Land Office, but the work was much more demanding. "Bill Bales believed that if he paid you a salary, he owned you for the whole 24-seven," Bruce said. "We worked on Sunday. Worked late at night. Sometimes to get an order out, we'd work till one or two in the morning."

Despite the arduous conditions, the job rekindled a couple of Bruce's long-time interests. Little vehicles and manufacturing in general had always held a special fascination. Bales's golf carts were mundane as mud, but being in intimate contact with the process of their production got Bruce's creative juices flowing. He started to envision a vehicle of his own, a unique design that could serve as more than a golf cart.

Bill Bales was not a pleasant character to work for, but Bruce managed to draw a bit of inspiration from his dynamic way of getting things done. Bruce realized that if he was ever going to achieve his larger goal of moving his airplane designs beyond the experimental stage, he would have to adopt some of the more effective methods of his otherwise obnoxious employer. So he conceived a business plan. He would develop his own vehicle and set up a factory. He knew the process. He knew the ins and outs.

But this venture would just be a stepping-stone. After a few years, he could sell the profitable operation or turn it over to trusted employees and then direct most of his time and surplus funds toward designing, building, and promoting his airplanes.

* * *

The vehicle Bruce K. Hallock dreamed up was called the Motor Rickshaw. The initial inspiration had been prompted by his involvement with the golf cart manufacturing operation, but his design set out in a different direction — or several directions. The Rickshaw was conceived as a souped-up, motorized wheelchair, something that could be used by handicapped individuals on the sidewalk. Then this concept fell by the wayside as he incorporated other ideas that expanded the possible uses, ultimately resulting in a more robust vehicle.

Although the Motor Rickshaw's purpose evolved, the basic configuration remained unchanged. Bruce's vehicle resembled a traditional manpowered rickshaw only to the extent that it was essentially a cart with one seat supported by two large, spoked wheels. But instead of a human runner, an engine was mounted in front directly over a transmission, which drove a pair of close-set, small-diameter wheels. Steering was managed by turning this entire engine-transmission assembly — originally by means of a tiller, later by a steering wheel.

Bruce's Motor Rickshaw differed significantly from the so-called auto rickshaws used as taxies in many parts of Asia. The Motor Rickshaw featured front-wheel drive and did not have a separate seat for the driver. It was designed to carry two persons side by side on a fiberglass bench seat. The center-mounted steering wheel allowed the vehicle to be driven from either side, and both sides were provided with accelerator and brake peddles. A cargo area was behind and under the seat. A bulbous fiberglass cowling covered the engine-transmission assembly, and comely fiberglass fenders skirted the rear wheels. A surrey-style, fringed canopy shaded the riders.

The Rickshaw was licensed as a motorcycle in Texas. A six-hp, four-cycle Lauson-Tecumseh engine propelled it at speeds up to 25 mph. It had a belt-driven centrifugal clutch, so no shifting was required — except to put it in reverse. Since the two drive wheels were spaced closely together, no differential was necessary. The transmission was adapted from a heavy-duty garden tiller. Another interesting feature was a tow bar that could be inserted between the two front wheels and secured to the frame. The front end could then be lifted up and clamped to a standard trailer hitch on the back of an automobile. (The sales brochure advised removing the surrey top before towing at roadway speeds.)

Motor Rickshaw sales brochure.

Aside from the engine, drive train, and certain details, Bruce designed and built the entire vehicle himself. Both the engine module and the carriage itself underwent myriad tests and modifications. Once he was satisfied with the prototype, Bruce produced jigs and fiberglass molds, and set up a factory in East Austin. He hired a couple of employees and even pressed his sons into service. The steel frames, fiberglass seats, and other parts began to multiply. By late 1963 a fleet of the cherry-red Motor Rickshaws was ready for market.

The design had come a long way from the original notion of a sidewalk-compatible vehicle. Service as a golf cart was nixed when

Bruce learned that the Motor Rickshaw's narrow rear tires would not be allowed on the manicured turf of most links. But other possible markets abounded. Anticipated customers included resorts, large motor courts, retirement villages, curriers, and individuals wanting to dash around town in something a bit unusual.

To expand the Motor Rickshaw's utility, Bruce made trailers. There was a two-wheel cargo trailer consisting of a flat bed with removable sides. And there was the passenger trailer, which was simply a motorless Motor Rickshaw body. Any number of these passenger trailers could be yoked together into a train, which created a stunning spectacle coming down the road.

A couple of variations on the basic Motor Rickshaw also emerged from the little factory on East First Street. An electric-powered version was developed. Batteries occupied most of the cargo area, but from the outside, this quieter model looked just like its gasoline-powered brother. Bruce also produced a variation called the Minicab, which looked quite different but was essentially

Motor Rickshaw and Hallock family, circa 1963. Left to right: Enid, Gary, Mark, Bruce G., Don, Bruce K.

Bruce and Enid in Motor Rickshaw train.

a more streamlined version of the basic Motor Rickshaw. The Minicab featured a rigid roof, windshield, and streamlined cowling that did not turn with the engine-transmission unit.

The company Bruce created to build and market his vehicles was called Aerosphere, a name with an intentional aviation implication. Aerosphere would be the umbrella under which he would henceforth conduct all of his business activities; and his main business would always be airplanes. The Motor Rickshaw was to be a stepping-stone to greater things — a means to an end.

But the Motor Rickshaw did not sell well, and by the mid 1960s, the little red and white vehicles no longer figured into Bruce's long-term plans. Nevertheless the Rickshaws had made an impression locally, and they continued plying neighborhood streets for decades to come.

Chapter 11
BUILDING A BETTER AIRPLANE

Right after returning from the Latin America adventure in 1960, even before going to work for Lyndon Johnson, Bruce had started designing a couple of new tailless airplanes.

The HT-2 had been imagined before the war as a tailless twin engine, but Bruce had only sketched some ideas. Now having recently returned from a journey through regions lacking modern infrastructure, he hit upon the idea of developing the design as a small cargo plane. He dubbed it the Caravan, and wrote that it would be "for use in areas where an inexpensive, rugged, and simple airplane is needed to operate from poor airports and compete with difficult ground transportation." (It should be noted that Bruce Hallock's Caravan predated the unrelated Cessna design of the same name by several years.)

The rear end of the Caravan's fuselage would open upward, allowing easy access to the large hold. The airplane was intended to carry 3,000 pounds of bulky cargo, even a small automobile. With a fixed gear and two wing-mounted engines of approximately 500 horsepower each, the Caravan would cruise at about 170 mph. Bruce's original drawings indicated pusher engines, but he later settled on a tractor configuration. Either way, given the short tail moment, Bruce later admitted, the plane would have been difficult to handle in the event of an engine failure.

The HT-2 Caravan never progressed beyond preliminary design studies. But the other project initiated about the same time would go considerably further.

HT-2 Caravan display model featuring rear cargo hatch.

* * *

The HT-3 was conceived as a far more ambitious design than either the Road Wing or the Caravan. Rather than build an airplane that would compete directly with established types, Bruce proposed a forward-looking design that would define a class all its own. He wanted to set a new standard in the swiftly developing business aviation market with which he was now intimately familiar.

Bruce noted that high-performance single-engine airplanes were rapidly gaining wider acceptance among business fliers. Thanks to modern electronics and growing confidence in engine reliability, these airplanes were flying on instruments in greater numbers every year. He conducted an analysis of the high-end single-engine market and found that a "gap" existed among the array of current bestsellers. In a detailed proposal aimed at prospective investors, Bruce stated:

> I see a gap—a real need for a single-engine plane carrying five passengers in a "move around size" cabin at 200 mph. A plane aimed toward capacities, performance, and price above a Bonanza, but not so expensive or complex as the light twins. A plane, and this is important, that is not only competitive by today's standards but that is designed from inception to advance through a development program—a turboprop engine, twin engines, small jet engines, cabin pressurization, boundary layer control, radar, and other advancements.

The gap was currently being awkwardly bridged by souped-up versions of airplanes (some of them light twins) that had begun as more simple and less expensive machines—namely the Beechcraft Bonanza, the Cessna 210, the revived Navion, the Bellanca Cruisemaster, the Meyers 200, and the Piper Comanche. But none of these contemporary offerings, Bruce asserted, could be "stretched" to incorporate all the benefits of the technological progress currently at hand and soon to come. Furthermore all these airplanes, because of their basic configurations, lacked important conveniences and passenger-comfort features. These shortcomings, Bruce was convinced, restricted future development and hindered sales.

To meet the need he had identified, Bruce envisioned a sleek new tailless pusher with fully retracting landing gear. He proposed an airplane that would "outclass the competition for years." It would be "designed from the beginning to incorporate the quality, performance, and safety features expected of an all-weather business plane." He would offer "the quietest, roomiest, fastest, and most advanced light plane on the market—carrying five people in pressurized comfort at high altitudes over the weather at airline speeds." At first Bruce called his new design the HT-3 Aero King, but soon changed the name to Aero Wing.

Aero King display model built in 1960 or '61. Propeller shroud later abandoned as the design underwent numerous alterations and was renamed the Aero Wing.

The Aero Wing would be constructed primarily of riveted aluminum. But from the beginning, Bruce also intended to incorporate structural plastics as these materials were further developed. "The design seems uniquely suited to the eventual molding of large sections," he wrote.

For Bruce aerodynamics and aesthetics were one and the same. He liked to say that a good-looking airplane was a good-flying airplane. And he believed the Aero Wing's graceful lines flowed directly from the design's inherent efficiency.

In his technical description, he cited several aerodynamic justifications for his choice of the tailless pusher configuration. The design featured fewer component parts, which resulted in a lower minimum drag coefficient than could be achieved with other configurations. And since the value of minimum drag coefficient significantly affects performance characteristics such as speed, rate of climb, and service ceiling, the Aero Wing would be a more efficient

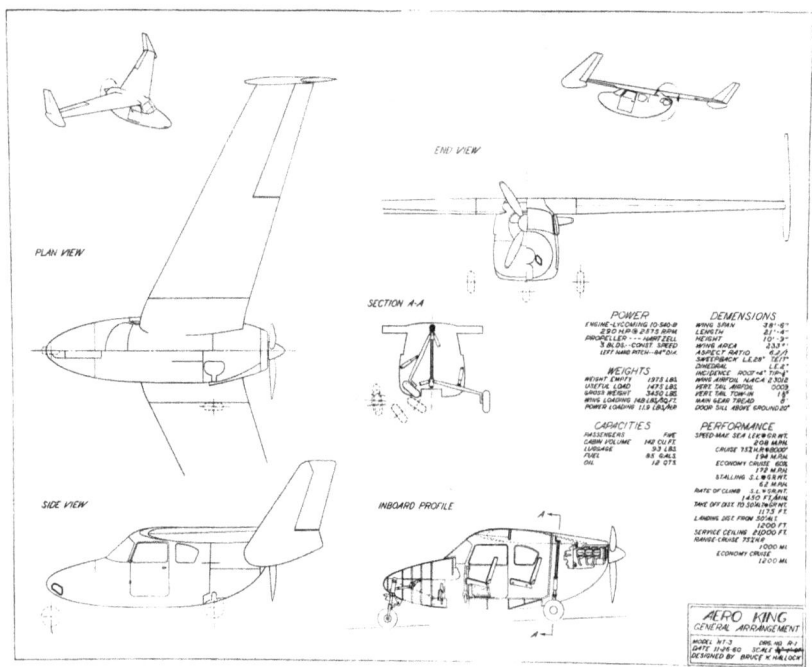

Original (1960) three-view drawings of the Aero King, later called the Aero Wing.

airplane. In addition the pusher propeller's slipstream, operating in an area away from any components of the airplane, would offer no interference drag and skin friction. Fewer component parts, he noted, would mean less need for maintenance, lower weight, and lower production costs. Additional bonuses realized from the pusher power installation would include a quieter cabin and reduced effect on stability and control due to power changes. The low wing loading and power loading, he concluded, would further contribute to the Aero Wing's superior performance.

Although these technical factors were compelling all by themselves, Bruce had additional considerations in mind. He wanted to offer a basic design that could be further developed over many years. In a letter to a friend and associate, he wrote: "At one time my interest concentrated heavily on extolling the tailless idea. But now I see this design as a much broader concept uniquely able to incorporate a host of new ideas to advance the general aviation product." In his formal proposal to potential investors, he emphasized the tailless pusher configuration's "greater opportunity to include, develop, and extend more desirable features of flight performance and passenger appeal."

Passenger appeal was to be a big selling point for the Aero Wing. The airplane would offer more than striking lines and a unique profile. Bruce's experience as an executive pilot had made him acutely aware of some of the daunting human factors confronting lightplane passengers. And his proposal vividly addressed these issues:

> I have witnessed many occasions where owning or even flying in single-engine planes has been vetoed because of the awkward contortions required to enter and leave the small cabin. The airplane is both a travel convenience and a prestige symbol, but its appeal in both realms is dampened before it leaves the ground when the passenger is asked to climb up on a landing gear into a door nearly three feet off the ground — or to climb on a spindly step, over the

wing and through a "manhole type" door. No single-engine airplane marketed today has a cabin that is more commodious than the midget European automobiles. Fancy molded plastics, foam rubber, and plush upholstery are offered as substitutes for plain old room.

So here is a primary consideration: the physical arrangement of the AERO WING offers an automobile's invitation, not a challenge, to enter. A single unobstructed step, without ducking under a wing, and the passenger enters through a large door. The cabin compares in size and comfort with his automobile. He may move freely during flight from the front to the rear seat. The view from the windows is less obstructed than from any other airplane [*thanks to the sweptback wings*]. Because the engine and the propeller follow behind, he is always moving away from these fatiguing noise makers.

And in another promotional document, he summed it up like this: "My airplane design has emerged from the passenger compartment outward as opposed to a philosophy that begins with the final machine into which people are stuffed."

* * *

Developing the Aero Wing was going to require considerably greater resources than had the Road Wing, but Bruce K. Hallock still wanted to do it himself, and perhaps his reasons weren't entirely rational. For years, he had nurtured a dream of starting his own aircraft company. He had drawn inspiration from the likes of Glenn Curtiss, Eddie Stinson, Donald Douglas, C. G. Taylor, and a host of other aviation pioneers who had started small and almost single-handedly turned their ideas into profitable and influential industries. But with few exceptions, this was not how airplanes were designed and built in the second half of the twentieth century. The industry had matured, and the freewheeling days of the independent designer-entrepreneur were mostly finished. More and more, commercially successful airplanes were being designed and developed by teams of engineers and other specialists working within the context of large corporate structures.

But Bruce focused on the exceptions to the rule. It was still possible for one man to forge his brilliant vision into a spectacular reality. And Bruce was possessed of enormous ambition and a resilient confidence in his own ability to do just about anything he set his mind to.

So he sought investors. Raising venture capital was not something with which he was familiar—but he gave it a shot. He developed a compelling proposal and detailed budget, which included expenses for such items as renting space, buying equipment and material, and hiring necessary help. Initially he estimated project development costs at $125,000 to be spread out over two years. Even in 1961 dollars, this figure was incredibly low. Although Bruce's ability to accomplish more with less was legendary, he was soon persuaded to revise his estimate upward.

Among the possible backers that he approached was Bert Beveridge, his old employer in Flint, Michigan. Bruce suggested a partnership. "After FAA certification," he wrote, "we could offer the entire project for sale at a handsome profit or as an alternative we might begin production by contracting with some large aircraft modification shop." Beveridge politely declined, explaining that his money was all tied up, and anyway such "pioneering" endeavors were outside of his area of experience and comfort. However, he did offer a few suggestions:

> It would seem to me a venture such as you propose has to be a "syndicate" deal by aviation enthusiasts or a project by a plane manufacturer with research funds or an outfit with a subsidy. To engineer, develop, and market a new product today is a rough one in any line and would take a lot of money. Frankly I think your plan is a much bigger financial

project than you have outlined. Wouldn't you be wiser to try to tie in with a going concern and sell your ideas and experience to them?

Bruce mulled over Beveridge's comments. He was not inclined to relinquish control of his project by "tying in with a going concern." But he eventually came up with a more realistic budget and two-phase development program. Phase One would consist of the completion of one prototype airplane and approximately 20 hours of evaluative flight testing. This initial flight testing was intended only to identify areas where major redesign might be necessary. These first tests would help provide the plan for approaching FAA certification of the aircraft for production. Some static tests would also be performed. He estimated this phase would take two years and about $211,000. It was still a modest estimate, but Bruce assumed that he'd be doing a lot of the work himself.

Phase Two would concentrate on meeting FAA certification requirements under Part 23, "Normal Category Aircraft," which allows an aircraft to be sold to the public and assures that it meets all standard requirements concerning stability, control, methods of construction, materials, and safety. Bruce believed that at least one more flyable test airplane would have to be built to reflect the many structural modifications and refinements that would be impractical to incorporate in the original prototype. Both airplanes, however, could participate in the flight-test portion of the certification program. Bruce conceded that time and cost for this phase would be difficult to forecast, but he pointed out that typical airplanes in the recent past had required one to two years and expenditures of around $700,000 to complete the certification program.

Another person Bruce consulted was Koert Voorhees, husband of Enid's first cousin and a successful entrepreneur. Koert took an interest in the project, and over the course of several years, the two men carried on a lively exchange of letters and visits. Koert's free-ranging inquiries and outside-the-box suggestions probably helped

Bruce crystallize his thinking. Through Koert, Bruce connected with more prospective investors. One man offered this sage advice: "My experience tells me that you should double whatever you think it will take." According to Koert, Bruce got a quizzical look on his face and replied, "Well, yes, but I've already done exactly that." Many expressed interest in the unique project, but ultimately no venture capital materialized.

* * *

Bruce's inability to attract serious backers did not stop him from moving ahead with the project. Much preliminary work could be done on a shoestring. And he still hoped to eventually obtain the funds necessary to see the project through, or perhaps sell the design to an established manufacturer.

The Aero Wing proceeded through several design iterations. Looking for ways to cut development costs, Bruce turned to the Aero Commander, a sleek, high-wing light twin that already possessed many of the cabin features he was looking for. He investigated the possibility of using the Aero Commander's front fuselage section, whose contours and dimensions were nearly ideal. Taking the Commander's cabin and nose, relocating the door, and integrating the unit into his own design offered some attractive advantages—namely big savings in time, engineering, and the expense of producing a prototype airplane for FAA certification. Such production refinements as molded windshields, metal pieces stamped into compound shapes, metal castings, control column, seats, panel trim, etc., would be ready-made. Bruce believed that incorporating these premanufactured elements would also help him avoid the "amateur look" that often stigmatized low-budget development. His slant on this plan was as follows: "Nobody could assert that the Aero Wing is a modified Commander, but using their cabin section identifies it with a respected quality product."

To investigate the feasibility of this scheme, Bruce visited the Aero Commander factory and inspected their production of the needed section. For the prototype he thought he could acquire the fuselage of a salvaged Commander, but upon reaching the production stage, he would need a reliable supply. He was happy to learn that the company could fulfill his initial needs.

Bruce's early drawings and solid-wood scale model of the Aero Wing assumed the incorporation of the Aero Commander body, but after pursuing the idea for a while he ultimately abandoned it. For one thing, a salvageable Aero Commander fuselage could not be found. When such an airplane is wrecked, the fuselage almost always suffers major damage. But more important, his design ideas began to evolve beyond what the Aero Commander components had to offer. Furthermore he came to realize that he possessed the knowledge and skills needed to build his own high-quality fuselage.

He started with a plywood mockup consisting of a half fuselage mounted on a vertical surface. This full-size mockup helped him lay out control system mechanics, design the landing-gear retraction system, work out cabin dimensions (headroom, legroom, etc.), and resolve certain details of construction. About this time he decided to incorporate a Learjet-style clamshell door, hinged at top and bottom, with the bottom portion incorporating the steps. Then after

Aero Wing fuselage under construction with mocked up nose. B. K. Hallock and son Gary inside, mid 1970s.

further refining the design, he began construction of the actual aluminum fuselage.

* * *

The question of the Aero Wing's power plant remained a major variable throughout its long development history. Initially Bruce planned to use the 290-hp Lycoming IO-540-B1, at least for the prototype. Predicting future performance enhancements, he calculated that a 450-hp reciprocating engine would allow the Aero Wing to cruise above 20,000 feet at over 250 mph. And in 1970 he wrote: "As follow-on development, the design can accommodate a single turbine engine or (the most exciting prospect) three smaller engines driving a single propeller." This tri-motor arrangement did not exist anywhere in the real world, but he had his eye on an Allison turbine that geared two 250-hp engines to one shaft.

The idea of a twin-engine package driving one prop through a clutch arrangement was appealing for several reasons. It would allow twin-engine power and safety for takeoffs and landings and the option of single-engine economy while cruising. Bruce imagined several different arrangements for this, including stacked and side by side. The Aero Wing's capacious rear engine compartment opened up many possibilities that were closed to designs with tightly cowled front-mounted engines. Perhaps the most curious variation on this theme involved the use of two Chevrolet V8 engines. The automobile engines were proposed only for the experimental prototype in order to reduce development costs.

But ultimately Bruce moved away from the twin-engine-one-propeller idea. One reason was the complexity of the clutching mechanism: it would have entailed more extra work than he wanted to tackle during the project's preliminary development. Also many of the new aero engines coming onto the market looked very promising. His favorite was the Pratt & Whitney PT6, a popular turboprop. But the PT6 was expensive for a developer on a tight budget. So by the 1990s, Bruce was leaning toward the 600-hp Orenda, an aluminum V8, which would turn a state-of-the-art, four-blade scimitar propeller. Still his thoughts about the airplane's future development spanned a wide variety of possibilities, including stretching the cabin and installing small jet engines. But that would have to wait. First he needed to get the project off the ground.

* * *

In addition to the early static display model of the Aero Wing, Bruce later built a one-fifth-scale flying model. This was in lieu of a wind-tunnel model. Although strictly for testing purposes, the model received the same meticulous care that Bruce lavished on all the model airplanes he'd ever built. It was beautifully constructed of balsa and foam and reflected his latest design ideas, including Fowler flaps, tandem dual wheels on the main gear, and dual wheels on the nose gear. This test model was designed to be fitted with radio controls and either flown or mounted on the hood of a car or truck so that it could swivel and pivot in all planes. In the latter arrangement, the vehicle would be driven at velocities simulating flight speeds while a passenger operated the radio controls to test the model's performance and characteristics. Although the proposed tests were never conducted, the model provided certain insights that helped in refining the Aero Wing's design.

As the years passed, the Aero Wing underwent several design changes. While the basic concept remained relatively constant, numerous other features were added, removed, or reconfigured — mostly in an effort to improve aerodynamics and overall efficiency.

A prominent component of the original design was a propeller shroud. This device — especially well suited to the pusher configuration — was intended to improve static and low-speed thrust. The shroud would have been attached at two points on the wings' trailing edges. Later design changes precluded the use of the propeller shroud. Bruce considered this trade-off acceptable, considering the slight advantage the device would have provided. Nevertheless, the shroud had lent a distinctive look to the early artist's conceptions of the airplane.

To help reduce drag at high speeds, Bruce wanted to use a modern laminar-flow airfoil section on the Aero Wing. However, because of the relatively poor low-speed characteristics of such wings, he was reluctant to do so at first. He struggled with this dilemma until the early 1970s, when he hit on the idea of adding small, high-lift canard wings. These surfaces would extend from either side of the Aero Wing's nose to improve low-speed lift and stability. And since the appendages were not compatible with the high-speed end of the performance profile, the little wings would be retractable. Flush panel covers behind the canard wings slid open, and the canard wings pivoted at their roots, folding back inside the nose. Then the covers slid forward again, hiding the canards, except for a smooth "knuckle" protruding from either side of the nose. This addition required a lengthening of the airplane's nose and an intricate arrangement of shafts, gears, cables, pulleys, and locks. But Bruce relished the challenge, and the finished mechanism was a marvel of ingenuity reminiscent of a Swiss watch. A flap-like, trailing-edge control surface also deflected downward when the canard wings were deployed. The canards would be used in conjunction with the main wings' Fowler flaps to increase lift and drag during takeoff and landing.

B. K. Hallock with Aero Wing test model. Note wing pods, Fowler flaps, and nose-mounted retractable canards.

Aero Wing's canards deployed. Note flush panel cover visible behind the right canard. The panels slide into place to conceal the slots into which the little wings fold.

At some point during the 1980s, Bruce added large pods to the wings about ten feet out from the roots. He suggested several possible functions for these appendages. Since they were longitudinally positioned over the center of gravity, the pods were well situated for carrying fuel or baggage (originally the fuel tanks were to be inside the wings). Another idea he entertained for a while was hinging the wings at the outside of the pods so they could be folded upward and over the back of the airplane. This folding scheme would effectively halve the airplane's 39-foot wingspan and save costly hangar space. If this were done, the pods would house the wing-folding mechanism.

But gradually another function for the pods emerged. Bruce became concerned about the weight that the wingtip-mounted vertical stabilizers and rudders added to the cantilever wings and the associated reinforcement required to support them. If he extended the pods rearward, they could support the fins and rudders with less overall structural underpinning. He also decided to add small horizontal control surfaces to the top of each vertical fin to work in concert with the elevons. And with the wingtips free of the vertical fins, winglets could be added. Winglets are nearly vertical extensions at the tip of each wing designed to reduce the lift-induced drag caused by vortices. With the vertical fins now protruding from the wing pods, the wing-folding idea was out, but the pods could still accommodate fuel tanks, luggage, lights, and even avionics such as radar. This modification significantly altered the airplane's profile, and some observers grumbled that the design had been over-refined at the expense of its simple beauty. Nevertheless, the change was set.

Although sound engineering judgement underlay each of these alterations, they all held up progress. Bruce spent enormous amounts of time working out geometries, designing fittings, and brooding over details. Meanwhile the years passed.

Mockup of Aero Wing's wing pod with appended rudder, 2005.

Partially mocked-up wing and pod with rudder, wingtip in foreground.

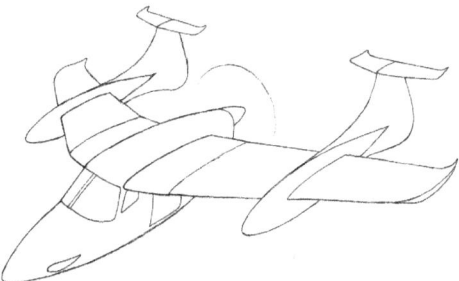
Aero Wing as it would have looked with rudders on the wing pods. Sketch by Don Hallock.

* * *

The star-crossed saga of the Aero Wing would continue until the end of Bruce K. Hallock's life. He never finished the prototype, yet for over four decades he held to the dream. Other projects came and went. Mundane concerns had to be dealt with. Life's inevitable trials intervened. And still he remained faithful to the vision of the Aero Wing. In a letter to his friend and confidant Koert Voorhees, Bruce wrote: "I have too much wrapped up in this airplane project to even consider shelving it for something else. I'll stick with it no matter what turn it takes." That was in 1971. By the beginning of the new millennium, the project had taken many turns and still remained far from rolling down the runway.

Why was the Aero Wing never finished? It wasn't really for lack of funds. Bruce eventually possessed sufficient means to at least complete the first prototype. Factors other than money came into play.

Bruce was a man of great talent and energy. He also possessed two other qualities that sometimes served him well and other times

Aero Wing under construction with test model hanging above. Mothballed Pterodactyl in background. Late 1990s.

held him back. The first was a kind of perfectionism, an unwillingness to proceed with a design before he had it fully refined. He was loath to turn out deficient or incomplete work—an admirable trait but also one that tended to slow him down. This was further exacerbated by his fertile mind, which was continually devising improvements, causing him to backtrack and reengineer work already completed. In the world of commerce, many products that are simply "good enough" go to market and succeed splendidly. Bruce didn't want his name associated with a mediocre airplane, and he seemed increasingly reluctant to produce even an experimental prototype that lacked refinement or exhibited any flaws.

The second problematic trait was his solitary tendency. He was certainly no recluse, but he preferred working alone, sometimes to the detriment of his own best interests. He tended to shy away from others who might be of assistance, especially in the area of marketing. Even though he acknowledged the need for help, the seeking of it seldom rose high among his near-term priorities. A strong self-reliant streak informed his approach to all his endeavors.

Aero Wing as it might have been. Painting by Don Hallock, mid-1970s.

These failings were not absolute. He could, after much cogitation, move forward on a project. And he did make sporadic efforts to cultivate contacts beyond the workshop. But ultimately none of this was enough.

When Bruce K. Hallock died in November 2005, the Aero Wing was little more than an intricate shell of a fuselage with one wing and some other appendages mocked up. The wistful drawings and earnest writings held mute testimony to the dream of a better airplane the world would never see.

Chapter 12

TOP SECRETS AND EMERGENCY LANDINGS

The decades of the Aero Wing project included many other activities. About the time the first Aero Wing mockup was taking shape, Bruce's flying career took off in a new direction. Across town the Defense Research Laboratory of the University of Texas at Austin was working on several contracts for the Navy. DRL had pulled together a team of dynamic intellects to tackle some of the complex challenges associated with missile guidance and target identification.

Much of this work involved airborne research and tests of specialized radar. For this purpose the Navy had provided the Lab with an SNB (Twin Beech). At first the Beech was piloted by Perry Hall Lisman, one of the Lab's head scientists. But as DRL's flying activities stepped up, the need for a dedicated pilot with a solid aeronautical engineering background became evident.

It happened that a cousin of Enid's, Don Lauderdale, was working at the Defense Research Lab as an electrical engineer. When the question of hiring a pilot arose, Don told his coworkers that he knew an excellent candidate. So it came to pass that Bruce K. Hallock underwent a background check, obtained the appropriate security clearance, and became the chief pilot for DRL.

A young technical staff assistant by the name of Ted Cloer, who had been riding in the copilot's seat with Perry Lisman, continued in that role when Bruce took over. "I was very happy when Bruce started flying that Twin Beech," Ted said. Lisman was a brilliant scientist and inventor, but his aviation background was not broad. He had been a Navy jet pilot, flying F9Fs, and was generally credited as a capable pilot — once the airplane was in the air. "His air work was very good," Ted said, "but he didn't really know the airplane or understand its mechanics."

Ted Cloer had always enjoyed flying but hadn't seriously considered becoming a pilot until he started riding with Bruce in the latter part of 1962. Within a few months, Ted purchased a Taylorcraft and, after a little instruction time with Bruce, he soloed. Ted quickly obtained his private license and then his commercial rating. Before long he was Bruce's regular copilot at DRL.

* * *

DRL often had several projects running concurrently. Most of the work that Bruce participated in involved tests of either missile guidance systems or new radar applications — or both. Typically antennas of various types were mounted on the airplane, and a team of scientists in the cabin would monitor the performance of the equipment. The scientific team was headed by Fred Beckner, who everyone seemed to agree was an outright genius. Fred usually rode in the airplane, keeping close tabs on the tests.

These projects required numerous trips to far-flung sites and some pretty hair-raising flying. Early on, Bruce and Ted took the Twin Beech up to Silver Springs, Maryland, where they participated in an extensive project in conjunction with Johns Hopkins University Applied Physics Laboratory.

The experiments required Bruce to fly head-on against a Piper Apache. The two airplanes were supposed to be vertically separated by 250 feet, the Piper above the Beech. Of course Bruce and Ted were vigilantly watching for the oncoming plane, but on a few occasions they hadn't seen anything when the radar man monitoring them from the ground announced: "Okay, you've passed each other." Ted, who claimed that his vision was excellent in those days, often *did* spot the rapidly approaching Apache — though he suspected the other pilot seldom saw them. On most passes they were off to one side or the other, but on one memorable occasion, they were dead-on course with a vertical separation of only about 50 feet.

The purpose of this daring exercise was to simulate a so-called "slow closure rate" in the testing of forward-looking antennas. To the pilots flying head-on, a closure rate of well over 300 mph may not have seemed slow, but the antennas being tested were for the Talos and Typhon guided missiles, which flew at supersonic speeds.

The Talos was an early ship-based surface-to-air and surface-to-surface missile that was in use between 1958 and 1979. The Typhon was a much faster and more advanced successor to the Talos that never saw active service. Both missiles had solid-fuel boosters and ramjet sustainers. Later, on one of their many trips to White Sands Missile Range, Bruce and Ted witnessed a couple of Talos test firings. Standing perhaps too close to the launch site, they would never forget the painful bone-jarring noise.

Bruce and Ted made numerous trips to Silver Springs and other sites on the East Coast. In addition to the missile radar testing, they also participated in studies to catalog the radar echo signatures of various ocean wave states and different types of "sea clutter." These missions involved flying back and forth over the ocean while the scientists in the plane's cabin compiled and compared the radar profiles of waves and the flotsam tossed thereon. Presumably the data could eventually be used by the Navy to help distinguish targets of interest from their surroundings on the ocean's surface. But the guys collecting the radar signatures had only a vague notion of the data's ultimate application.

Among the things the Navy was definitely interested in discerning on the sea's surface were signs of submarines. So as part of another project, the radar-laden Twin Beech spent many hours shadowing submarines off the Atlantic coast near Groton, Connecticut. The scientists were developing radar methods for detecting partially submerged conning towers, periscopes, and submarine wake turbulence. At the beginning of the project, Ted could usually spot the periscopes before Fred Beckner's instruments in the back of the plane. But as the scientists refined their detection methods, they began to win out over the copilot's extraordinary naked-eye vision, identifying the periscope up to 19 miles away.

* * *

Another project called for ground-based operators to visually spot the Twin Beech in order to train their radar on it. At the distances required, the task proved very difficult, even with binoculars. So someone proposed using a smoke system of the type used by skywriters and aerobatic flyers to help make the plane more visible. Ted Cloer took on the project. He contacted famed aerobatic pilot Frank Price of Waco, Texas, and learned about the fine points of producing trails of smoke in the sky. Then he bought a pump and some hydraulic line and proceeded, with Bruce's reluctant consent, to install a smoke system in the Twin Beech.

The Beech's 47-gallon nose tank was converted to hold corvis oil, the type of vegetable oil typically used for creating smoke trails. Ted ran a line from the nose tank to the right engine and put a receptacle in the exhaust manifold. Bruce wanted to be sure that the pump and oil line did not interfere with any vital linkages. He was also wary of modifications to the exhaust. So Ted proceeded carefully, seeking advice from local aircraft mechanics and doing all the work according to standard practices. In the end Bruce signed off on the installation — and he even came to like it. The system produced voluminous amounts of puffy, white smoke and succeeded in

The Lab's Twin Beech at White Sands Missile Range, Condron Field, 1965.

making the airplane readily visible at a great distance. Bruce had to admit it was fun to use.

* * *

Bruce worked for the Defense Research Laboratory on a consultancy basis—that is, he was not a regular employee. When he was on a trip, the hours were long and he was away for days and weeks at a time. But there was still sufficient free time to pursue other endeavors. So the Motor Rickshaw manufacturing and airplane building proceeded between projects. He would continue to fly for the Lab on and off for most of two decades.

In 1968, DRL was renamed Applied Research Laboratories. Bruce believed this change was an attempt to obscure the military nature of their work during an era of widespread antiwar sentiment. Whatever the case, everyone who worked at DRL/ARL just called it "the Lab."

In the early years, the schedule was very busy, and in 1965 the Lab acquired a second airplane for use in its numerous projects. It was a TC-47K, essentially a DC-3 fitted out as a navigational trainer (and the people at the Lab usually just called it "the DC-3"). The airplane was provided by the Navy under a bailment contract. Although operated by civilians, it was still a military airplane and had to be maintained and operated according to reams of Navy regulations, which referenced FAA regulations. But within a couple of years, the Navy actually transferred ownership to the Lab, and the DC-3's status changed to "public aircraft." This classification was possible because the University of Texas was a subdivision of a state government and the airplane was not used for commercial purposes and supposedly carried only "qualified" crew members and passengers. Public aircraft is the same category under which, for example, police department aircraft are operated. The classification also provided a certain amount of leeway for modifications and allowed maintenance by noncertified mechanics—like Bruce and Ted.

And modifications were certainly made. Over the years, various antennas, struts, pods, shrouds, and other appendages sprouted from the plane. Inside the cabin, racks of electronic equipment were installed. And to power all the equipment, three inverters put out 500 amps of alternating current. With everything running, it was noisy and hot inside—100 degrees was not unusual. Ted built scoops to pull in air, but the strong blast was uncomfortable. And much of the work required flying very low over the ocean where the incoming air was oppressively hot and damp. Surprisingly none of that plentiful amperage was ever used on air conditioning.

Early on, the DC-3 participated in further tests of the Talos nose-cone radar. The antennas were mounted on the airplane's underbelly. This arrangement exposed the equipment to dirt and grit during takeoffs and landings and even while taxiing around. The problem was particularly evident when they were flying out of White Sands Missile Range; the delicate antennas were literally being sandblasted.

Some sort of protective cover was needed. So a pod was fashioned, but its foam construction interfered with the radar signal. The next most expedient solution seemed to be a plexiglass radome covering the whole array. Sheets of clear plexiglass were pieced together and glued with chloroform and a strips of fiberglass tape. The multifaceted structure measured about 15 feet long by eight feet wide and about three feet deep. It was dubbed "the greenhouse," and the scientists were delighted that it was totally transparent to radar frequencies. But Bruce and Ted were not enthusiastic at all. Ted pointed out that the adhesives used were much weaker than the material itself, and he predicted that vibration would cause the assembly to break at the seams.

But objections were overruled, and Bruce and Ted took the greenhouse-adorned DC-3 up for a test flight. They flew out north of Austin. Judging by the way the airplane handled, the new addition didn't seem to induce too much turbulence—a good sign. Ted took the controls while Bruce went back in the cabin to have a look at the greenhouse through a periscope mounted in the floor. Everything seemed fine, so Ted took the plane up to 3,000 feet and pushed the speed up to 150 knots. Bruce was still peering at the structure when it suddenly vanished.

Back at Austin's Robert Mueller Municipal Airport, an air-traffic controller had trained his binoculars on the distant DC-3. The odd appendages and unusual maneuvers of the Lab's airplanes made them constant objects of interest. On this day the sun was glinting off something underneath the airplane. Then the controller did a double take as a shimmering rain fell from the plane.

In the DC-3's cockpit, Ted had felt a little lurch, but the event hadn't really made a big impression on him. Then Bruce returned from the cabin and calmly said, "Well, let's go back. It's gone."

At this point the two pilots didn't know if their airplane had suffered any damage, so they were anxious to land and check things out. About this time, an inquiry came in from the control tower: "Hey, were you all dropping something out there?"

Bruce and Ted exchanged wry looks. Then Bruce answered, "Well, not intentionally, but we're going back to get it."

And they did. Several people from the Lab immediately drove out to where the plexiglass had fallen. Although the area was rural, there were a few homes. The Lab employees went door to door, telling people that the stuff that had fallen from the sky was part of "a classified government project," and if they found any of it, they'd better turn it over right away. A woman who had picked up one of the panels and taken it inside for some use of her own reluctantly handed over her prize. Another section had fallen into a backyard and almost whacked a dog. And yet another was retrieved from the roof of a house. "Actually what we were doing was collecting (and concealing) evidence," Ted admitted years later.

Luckily the incident generated no legal repercussions, and afterwards very little was said about the ill-fated greenhouse around the

Lab. Bruce eventually devised a proper fiberglass enclosure to protect the antennas, and the program continued.

* * *

Both the Twin Beech and the DC-3 were kept in Ragsdale's Flying Service hangars on the north side of Robert Mueller Airport. During the mid and late 1960s, both planes were in continuous use. While one airplane was away on a project, technicians would be refitting the other. As the volume of work tapered off in the 1970s, the Lab let go of the Twin Beech, but the DC-3 continued in use into the late '70s.

Another significant modification to the DC-3 was the mounting of two Bullpup missile hulls beneath the center section of the wing. The Lab was not testing the Bullpup itself, which was an early air-to-surface, command-guided missile. Instead they were using the decommissioned missile hulls to house short-pulse radar. They were perfect for the purpose.

Bruce and Ted mounted the Bullpup hulls on a set of well-braced struts. The struts were attached to fittings right below the fuel tanks, which raised some concern. If the plane were ever forced to

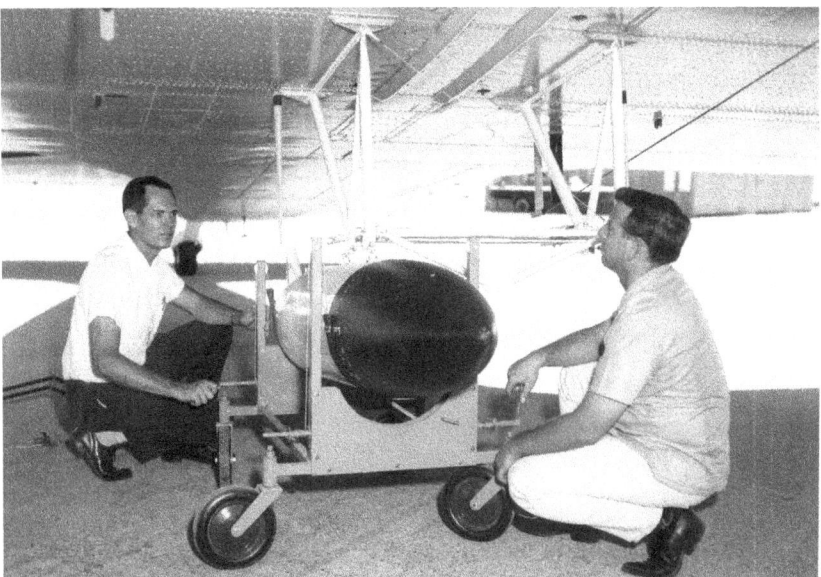

Bruce and Ted Cloer mounting a Bullpup hull under the DC-3, 1966.

land with the gear retracted, the missile hulls and their supports would hit the ground, and the whole assembly would be pushed up through the fuel tank—not a good scenario. So Ted rigged a hydraulic release that would allow the pilot to drop the missile pods and their struts in the event of an emergency. Thankfully, no such emergency ever arose.

Bruce and Ted flew the scientific team out to many distant locales. The work was sometimes tedious but always interesting. And most of it was classified. When they were at White Sands Missile Range working on the Talos and Typhon missile radar, their flight times, routes, and altitudes were strictly controlled. And the team never knew when they were going to fly or for how long, so they had to be ready to go day and night. They were repeatedly cautioned to keep quiet about the work.

Bruce never disclosed any secrets or otherwise compromised national security, but he sometimes exhibited a rather cynical and even mocking attitude toward authority. And he seemed to enjoy bending the rules. In this spirit, he sometimes invited Enid to come along on the Lab trips. If anyone were to ask, she was a "crew member"—but no one asked or even seemed to notice. One time Enid was aboard when the DC-3 landed at Naval Air Station Oceana in

Bruce with fiberglass radar-antenna enclosure, which he designed and built for the DC-3's underbelly.

Virginia Beach. The project involved some radar work in conjunction with activities at the nearby air-combat maneuvering range. Bruce and Ted stepped out of the airplane looking like (according to Enid) "a couple of scrounges." The officials thoroughly checked the two men's papers, but they paid no attention to her. Enid said she felt totally invisible. Apparently her presence was so incongruous that the people in charge either couldn't or didn't want to make sense of it. Enid followed everyone into a large trailer that served as some kind of command center where alert technicians tended banks of video monitors—and no one ever said a word to her.

The petty concerns of military brass and other officials also seemed to elicit a certain mischievousness from Bruce. One time when he had the DC-3 in San Diego, a man started nosing around the odd-looking airplane. Bruce approached, and the man snippily identified himself as an FAA official and asked to see inside the airplane. Bruce took an instant dislike to the fellow and replied, "Sorry, no, it's classified—secret." The frustrated official backed off, and right after that a group of eager schoolchildren appeared. Cheerfully Bruce invited them all to have a look inside the airplane.

B. K. Hallock with the Lab's DC-3 (TC-47K) in Austin, Texas.

* * *

Probably the most exotic locale that Bruce visited while working for the Applied Research Labs was Aruba, a small Dutch island in the Caribbean off the coast of Venezuela. Aruba offered lots of sunshine and a fairly constant wind of around 25 mph, ideal for a particular phase of the Lab's ongoing sea-clutter studies. But the flying was hot and rough. Bruce and Ted flew low over the ocean while Fred Beckner and his scientific team took low-glancing-angle measurements with X- and C-band radar and confirmed their results with a laser profilometer.

One day when the team was out working over the waves, a call came in from Aruba air-traffic control. A Curtiss C-46 loaded with frozen chickens had departed Puerto Rico headed for Aruba, and just beyond the midpoint of the 450-mile flight over open ocean, the plane had lost one of its two engines and was not maintaining altitude. Speaking in heavily accented English, the Dutch controller asked the Americans if they would please use their radar equipment to track the stricken aircraft. Poor radio reception, background noise, and the language barrier thwarted an explanation of the fact the specialized radar aboard the DC-3 was totally useless for tracking airplanes. Nevertheless, Bruce and the others decided to try to visually spot the cargo plane and perhaps escort it in. If the C-46 went down, they might at least identify the location to aid rescue efforts.

So Bruce headed out in the direction from which the crippled airplane was coming. The cargo plane was reportedly flying at less than 100 feet above the water. Bruce climbed up to 3,000 feet to get some perspective, and everyone started scanning the seascape below. Broken clouds prevented a clear view, but Bruce didn't want to go any lower because he was supposedly on a collision course with the approaching plane, which could have been flying higher than reported.

Ted was the one who spotted it — a tiny shape that flashed between a gap in the clouds below. "We're exactly lined up with them," Ted said, "I mean *exactly*."

Bruce executed a tight, descending U-turn and gave chase. It took a while to catch up. The Lab's DC-3, with all its drag-inducing antennas and radar-housings, had to go to high-cruise power to keep up with the C-46 flying on one engine. By this time the cargo plane was down to about 25 feet above the water and, thanks to ground effect, maintaining altitude. Bruce flew alongside. The pilots in the C-46 cockpit had put on their life vests. The pilot spoke Spanish and the copilot Vietnamese, so there wasn't much radio communication—just an encouraging wave.

By this time, they were only about 50 miles out from the Aruba airport. Bruce looked at his fuel gauges and realized that, if the C-46 somehow had a mishap on the runway and couldn't be cleared off right away, there would be no place for him to set down. So he radioed the control tower and asked for permission to come in ahead of the cargo plane. The reply came back clearly enough: "Sorry, these guys have declared an emergency, so you'll have to wait for them."

Bruce circled the field and watched. The C-46 came straight in, skimming so low that the pilot actually had to pull up and climb a little bit to reach the runway. But the frozen chickens arrived safely. And minutes later the radar-festooned DC-3 also touched down.

The event was big news in Oranjestad, Aruba's main city. The local newspaper carried a front-page story describing how the intrepid scientists from the United States, who happened to have been in the air at the time the stricken aircraft was en route to Aruba, used their powerful radar to find the airplane and escort it in. Fred Beckner saw the story first, and he told the others: "Now don't you all say anything to contradict this." And no one did.

* * *

There were two trips to Aruba, and getting there and back proved at least as interesting as being there. To reach the little island in the Netherlands Antilles, the DC-3 traced a route down through Mexico and Central America and then east over the southern Caribbean. On one of the trips down, the team refueled in Tapachula, Mexico, which is in the southernmost corner of the country, near the border with Guatemala. The Mexican military authorities who operated the airport were notoriously strict. But the U.S. team had special clearance, and after much scrutinizing of papers and thumping of rubber stamps, all was found to be in order. So they refueled, ate lunch, exchanged pleasantries with the officials, and took off for San Salvador, their next stopover. But a huge thunderstorm soon arose in their path, and Bruce had no choice but to return to Tapachula.

This time it was as if they'd landed in an entirely different place. Opening the airplane door, the travelers were greeted by a squad of young soldiers with automatic rifles. The same officials who had so cordially facilitated their stopover less than two hours earlier now informed the U.S. citizens that they were not authorized for another landing in Mexico. Furthermore, according to their interpretation of regulations, foreign intruders must be held at gunpoint until matters could be resolved.

As the group waited in the terminal, Ted Cloer grew uncomfortable staring at the rifle muzzles and inquired whether or not the weapons were on safety. The Mexicans gave him an uncomprehending look. But after the question became clear, the soldiers exchanged knowing chuckles, and one who spoke fair English replied with a shrug, "This gun, it got no safety." Ted, who had some knowledge of the AR-15 rifle, took a closer look. Sure enough — the weapons had been modified and lacked safeties.

Efforts to communicate with the United States via telephone were unsuccessful. The situation was only resolved when Fred Beckner, who happened to be a ham radio operator, was allowed to use the radio in the airplane to send a Morse code message back to Austin. Someone at the Applied Research Labs then made the necessary diplomatic arrangements, and clearance was issued.

A similar situation arose on a return trip from Aruba when the DC-3 landed in Guatemala City. An official simply misread the travel document that granted clearance for a refueling stopover, and the airplane was impounded. This time the crew was not held at gunpoint, but under a kind of house arrest that restricted them to the area around the airport. Eventually the scientific team was allowed to continue their homeward journey aboard a National Guard airplane that happened to be there. But Bruce and Ted, the pilots who had made the alleged unauthorized landing, were detained. A process to obtain diplomatic clearance was set in motion, but the affair dragged on for a week. Finally, just as the diplomatic clearance was about to be issued, the Guatemalan officials realized their own mistake, and Bruce and Ted were abruptly informed that they were free to go.

"But it was really kind of worth it," Ted admitted later. The Guatemala City airport doubled as a military base, and every day Bruce and Ted watched World War II relics take to the air. Ted, who was too young to remember much about the war, enthusiastically enumerated the lineup: "They had Corsairs, Bearcats, Hellcats, P-51s, AT-6s, and PT-17s. They were all active, and they flew them every day. That was the first Bearcat I'd ever seen fly. And you wouldn't believe how well they took care of them! Their airplanes looked like show pieces."

Bruce also enjoyed the spectacle, but Ted's boyish gushing over these familiar old workhorses must have made him feel his age.

* * *

As an extension of the sea-clutter studies, the Lab began cataloging the radar signatures of various ships. This was done on so-called targets of opportunity. Any vessel encountered on the open water — from sailboats to Soviet trawlers — got buzzed and profiled by the low-glancing-angle radar. This work started in Aruba and continued on the West Coast off Los Angeles. The Navy even dummied up some fake Soviet-style guided-missile cruisers so the ARL team could record their radar signatures.

Bruce took the DC-3 to California several times. In San Diego he and the ARL team participated in experiments designed to take advantage of the tendency of electromagnetic waves — in this case, radar—to refract off the earth's atmosphere and follow the contour of the earth. The scientists referred to the phenomenon as the radar tunnel effect, and the military application under study involved detecting the presence of ships that were over the horizon. The experiments were conducted 150 to 200 miles out to sea. Bruce would drop down low and fly toward an aircraft carrier that was beyond the horizon so the scientists could test their radar. This project continued for about three weeks and was scheduled to go longer, but the aircraft carrier was unexpectedly called away.

Everyone was happy to go home early, so they fueled up the DC-3 and took off. Enid happened to be along on this trip, and a number of the scientists who normally traveled on the airlines were also on board. They refueled in El Paso and took off for Austin. At about 9,500 feet over the Sierra Diablo Mountains, a valve seat dropped out of a cylinder on the left engine. It smashed the piston and knocked off the top of the cylinder head. The rear sparkplug, which was still working, then set fire to the fuel coming from the intake manifold.

Bruce refrained from shutting down the engine. Despite the minor fire and the copious black smoke, the engine was still running. And as long as the engine was running, albeit weakly, the propeller would present less drag than it would if stopped and feathered. The fire didn't last long. The sparkplug was soon hammered over, and without a source of ignition, the blaze went out.

Bruce turned around and headed back for El Paso. Although they were nearly 100 miles out, there really wasn't another good choice. And Bruce felt they could make it. Ted radioed approach control and declared an emergency. They were losing altitude, but the terrain below was dropping away at about the same rate the plane was descending. Finally at 5,000 feet — about 1,000 feet above the ground—they were able to maintain altitude. Nevertheless, Bruce and Ted continually scanned the desolate landscape for emergency landing sites.

Just before the airport came into view, approach control called and asked if they could hold off while a 727 was vectored straight in. Ted replied by reminding them of the emergency and added, "You can do whatever you want with that 727, but we have the airport in sight, and we're flying straight to the airport. We're not turning one direction or the other. We're coming straight in." Perhaps at this point a brief smile crossed Bruce's face as he recalled their having to wait for the disabled cargo plane to land in Aruba.

A Bonanza pilot who had overheard the radio conversation flew alongside the DC-3. He called approach control and, confirming the urgent situation, announced that he was dropping back and giving up his own clearance to land ahead of the struggling aircraft.

The sputtering DC-3 came straight in and was quickly towed out of the way. The 727 and the Bonanza then landed in turn. Later Ted pointed out that, had the radar-tunneling project not been terminated early, "we would have been about 200 miles out over the ocean at between 50 and 100 feet when that engine let go." Bruce stoically concurred.

The engine could not be repaired, and Bruce, Ted, and Walter Birchfield (a machinist who worked for the Lab) ended up installing a new engine themselves.

Walter Birchfield and Ted Cloer replacing the DC-3's engine in El Paso.

* * *

By the late 1970s, the Lab no longer needed an airborne test bed, and in 1980 the DC-3 was sold to a broker in Fort Lauderdale, Florida, for $20,000. Bruce offered to deliver the airplane, and since it was still licensed as a public aircraft and not bound by the normal FAA operational rules, he gave his second son Don the opportunity to serve as copilot. Don had recently obtained his private license but was not multiengine rated. Nevertheless, Bruce felt he was good to go. So they went, with Don flying most of the way.

After delivering the airplane, Bruce and Don dined at a Fort Lauderdale restaurant. Bruce pulled out a crisp twenty-dollar bill and laid it on the table in front of his son. "That's for your takeoff in Austin," he said, and laid down another twenty. "And that's for your landing in New Orleans." A third twenty appeared. "And that's for your takeoff in New Orleans." A final twenty topped the stack. "And that's for your landing in Fort Lauderdale." Then Bruce smiled and said, "You see, flying really does pay."

No record remains of the amount Bruce was paid for the trip.

Don Hallock, DC-3 copilot.

Chapter 13

PTERODACTYL AND FRIENDS

At some point in the mid 1960s, Bruce K. Hallock decided he'd been without a personal airplane for long enough. More than sixteen years had passed since he'd sold his last Stinson Voyager in 1951. He'd been flying as a corporate pilot all this time, but he yearned for a plane of his own. And in late 1967 the time seemed right.

Bruce decided on a Navion, a sturdy, all-metal, low-wing, four-to-five-place monoplane with retractable tricycle landing gear. North American Aviation had originated the design for the burgeoning civilian market at the end of World War II. Astute observers discerned in the Navion echoes of the company's famous P-51 Mustang. In 1948, Ryan Aeronautical Company acquired the design and continued production into the early 1950s. Thereafter Navion passed though a series of corporate hands, with sporadic production of various models over the following decades.

Bruce admired the Navion's size, performance, looks, and reputation. He found a 1950 Ryan Navion B and scraped together the necessary $6,500. When he bought the plane, it was painted red and white, but Bruce soon had it redone in a striking gold scheme with white accents. He and Enid restored the plane themselves, completely refurbishing the interior and installing a new windshield and windows.

The Navion reawakened something in Bruce. Although still very much engaged with the Aero Wing project, he began to turn his thoughts toward sport aviation—flying for fun. The Aero Wing was aimed at the executive and corporate market, a sphere in which Bruce had been operating for years. He knew the field and was striving to make his mark there. He relished the demanding, long-term challenge of the Aero Wing. But the Navion answered a different need—a craving for the immediate and simple pleasure of flying. He purchased the Navion for the same reason he'd bought his first airplane back in 1945—not to make money, not to start a business, but just to *fly*.

The Hallocks were proud of their "new" Navion and took it on numerous cross-country trips. Bruce and Enid, sometimes accompanied by sons or friends, frequented fly-ins around the nation—Chino in California, Sun 'n Fun in Florida, and of course the big annual event in Oshkosh, Wisconsin, where in 1973, N5202K took the "Best in Class" award for restored planes over 250 hp.

A long-running problem with the Navion's starter puzzled Bruce for years, much to the continuing amusement of his friends. He could seldom get enough battery power to make the starter turn over adequately. He checked the battery. He checked the magnetos. And he even removed the starter and had it analyzed by an aviation electronics shop. Everything checked out fine, but the problem persisted. Meanwhile Bruce continued flying the airplane. To get it started, he often resorted to hand cranking.

Starting an airplane engine by hand is a fading art involving concentration and finesse. The Navion's geared engine made the task especially tricky, and pulling it through required considerable mus-

Navion N5202K in flight with Bruce K. Hallock at the controls.

cle. Bruce would position the Hartzell propeller just so and then signal to whomever was flying with him to flip the switch. Then he'd drape a rag over the trailing edge of the high blade to protect his hand and, with feet properly spaced and firmly planted, give a mighty heave as he stepped back. The Lycoming GO-435 usually coughed to life on the first try. The image of Bruce swinging the Navion's propeller remains vivid in many memories.

The mystery of the lazy starter was finally solved one day when Bruce was peering under the cowling for some unrelated reason. He called to a friend in the cockpit to press the starter button. A puff of smoke emerged from the wire grounding the engine to the airplane frame. He checked the connection. The wire was loose—and apparently it had been that way for years. He tightened it, and the problem was solved—mostly. Shortly afterwards Bruce also found that the high-tension leads from the magnetos to the sparkplugs were in poor condition and also leaking spark. So he put on a new harness, and the Navion's electrical troubles were over.

*　*　*

Although the Navion was for pleasure, any airplane or vehicle that crossed paths with Bruce eventually received the cool scrutiny of his engineer's eye. "How could this be better?" was the question that always seemed to run through his mind. And the Navion was not spared this sort of analysis.

One day Bruce was brainstorming with a young engineering graduate student named Charles Yant. They both admired the airplane, but they also recognized its shortcomings, namely a relatively slow cruising speed and certain aesthetic issues. These deficiencies put the Navion at a competitive disadvantage among its market contemporaries, such as the Beechcraft Bonanza. Bruce and Charles took a hard look at the Navion and realized that its weaknesses could easily be overcome. Furthermore the Navion's excellent reputation, enthusiastic following, and solid engineering made it a good candidate for a makeover.

After some deliberation, Bruce drafted a proposal that outlined an eleven-point plan to reengineer the Navion. The proposal was based on the newest version of the Navion called the Rangemaster. Introduced in 1960, the Rangemaster had already replaced the original sliding canopy with a door—a change Bruce applauded—and added wingtip fuel tanks to increase range. At the top of Bruce's to-do list was a redesign of the wing. He noted that the combination of airfoils used on the Navion dated back to the 1930s. "Those old high-drag airfoils," he pointed out, "[are] employed in no other airplane manufactured today, [and] are the most significant deterrent to ever creating a fast Navion." He advocated a modern laminar-flow airfoil while retaining the wing planform. This would allow the new wing to be manufactured in the original master jig using many of the same parts. Retaining the planform, including flap and aileron areas, would also "leave undisturbed many of the parameters that formed the basis for the structural and stability calculations

Hallock family and Navion circa 1971. Left to right: Mark, Don, Bruce K., Enid, Gary, and Bruce G.

and make FAA certification of the new wing simpler and less costly." Other proposed changes to the wing included:

- elimination of the external wingtip tanks, with auxiliary fuel capacity designed into the new high-speed wing;
- drooping ailerons, which deflect downward in conjunction with the flaps, to retain the low stalling speed of the original Navion;
- redesign of all flap and aileron hinges, brackets, and counterweights so that they are flush and do not protrude into the airstream; and
- new low-drag wingtips and improved wing-fuselage fillets.

Apart from the changes to the wing, the proposal recommended a redesign of the tail surfaces, a reconfigured cowling, an option for a supercharged engine, a pressurized cabin, and various human-factors engineering changes.

Bruce and Charles planned to submit the proposal to the current manufacturer of the Navion Rangemaster. The factory was in Seguin, Texas — not far from Austin — and Bruce's draft proposal concluded with an offer to head up the redesign effort. At the time, the Applied Research Laboratories' activities were in a lull, and Bruce was casting about for other work. He would have loved to take on the Navion redesign challenge. But he was also looking for ways to promote and finance his Aero Wing project, and having the successful redesign of the Navion on his résumé could not have hurt.

Alas, it was not to be. For reasons unknown, the proposal went nowhere. But this would not be the last airplane project that Bruce would envision — at least in part — as a way of raising funds for the Aero Wing.

* * *

Flying and maintaining his own airplane brought Bruce into closer contact with the fraternity of light-plane owners, and it wasn't long before he became involved with the preeminent organization of sport aviation enthusiasts: the Experimental Aircraft Association. Bruce had been aware of the EAA since its inception almost two decades earlier. In fact back in 1954 when he had just begun flying the de Havilland Dove for Bert Beveridge, Bruce happened to land at Curtiss-Wright Field in Milwaukee, Wisconsin. With a little time on his hands, he looked up a man named Paul Poberezny. The previous year Poberezny and 36 other enthusiasts had founded the EAA there in Milwaukee. Bruce was intrigued and wanted to know more.

The two men had lunch. Bruce told Poberezny about his then-unfinished Road Wing project and his future ambitions. Poberezny described his plans and hopes for his budding organization.

The Experimental Aircraft Association's purpose was to promote activities related to amateur-built or "homebuilt" aircraft. The word *experimental* may need some interpretation here. In general usage, something labeled as experimental has not been fully proven. The term suggests the testing of new ideas or a design-development program aimed at eventual commercial production—a fair description of the Road Wing's purpose. But the Federal Aviation Administration defines the category more specifically. In order to fly, all civilian aircraft must have an airworthiness certificate. Aircraft types produced by certified manufacturers undergo extensive testing to obtain so-called *standard* airworthiness certificates. But the FAA also issues *experimental* airworthiness certificates for a variety of purposes, including homebuilt aircraft. FAA rules require that such aircraft display the word EXPERIMENTAL on the door or cockpit. Most homebuilts are actually proven designs, even though they carry experimental airworthiness certificates. The designation simply represents their special legal category. And because regulations required the word to appear on so many homebuilt airplanes, Poberezny's organization chose to embrace *experimental* as a synonym for *sport* aviation.

Bruce did not join the EAA in the 1950s. The organization's efforts seemed focused on activities that held little interest for him: pedestrian modifications of standard airplanes (such as a twin-engine Piper Cub conversion), uninspired iterations of conventional designs (such as the Pietenpols, the Fly Baby, and the Volksplane), and the restoration of classics. Bruce had no quarrel at all with a club for people who wanted to build and fly airplanes for fun, but his ambitions were grander. He wanted to explore new designs and ultimately launch profitable ventures. He considered himself an experimenter in the literal sense and did not think of himself as a sportsman.

Two decades later Bruce's interests had broadened, and the EAA had also evolved. The organization had grown phenomenally, encompassing all manner of private aviation activities. Many members were pioneering innovative designs and using new materials and construction techniques. Interesting airplane kits and plans were being marketed to homebuilders, while the big manufacturers of light aircraft seemed to be mired in the past. Bruce became convinced that the EAA offered an excellent opportunity to advance his personal goals and perhaps contribute to the growth of civil aviation. So he joined the local Austin group, Chapter 187.

One of the founding members of EAA Chapter 187 was Tony Bingelis, who at the time was just beginning to achieve national acclaim through his "Sportplane Builder" column, which appeared in *Sport Aviation* magazine from 1972 through 1996. Over his long career, Tony also authored many books on the art of homebuilt aircraft. He was an early president of Chapter 187, and he and Bruce became good friends. By 1973 Bruce was taking a turn as chapter president.

* * *

Bruce made many friends and contacts through the EAA, and he remained a member for the rest of his life. The other members esteemed his knowledge and experience. And the encouragement and inspiration went both ways. Bruce found the surge of creative energy surrounding the club invigorating—so much so that he began to conceive a sport plane design of his own with an eye toward selling plans or kits to homebuilders.

He was encouraged in part by the likes of Jim Bede and Burt Rutan, both of whom were fomenting excitement among amateur builders. Jim Bede had virtually created the modern kit-plane market in the early 1970s when he introduced the BD-5, a very small single-seater. The BD-5's racy jet-like appearance and pusher configuration appealed to many. And the affordable price and stamped aluminum semi-monocoque fuselage made it a fairly accessible project. Although the BD-5 suffered from numerous problems, it stimulated many other designers to offer kits of their own.

In 1973 Burt Rutan began marketing a kit version of his Vari-Viggen, a tandem two-place pusher canard constructed of wood and fiberglass. Unlike the BD-5, the VariViggen used a real aircraft engine. Its unconventional configuration and jet-fighter styling made it a hit. And the great kit-plane race was on.

It probably surprised no one that the sport plane Bruce proposed was a tailless pusher. Actually he'd been kicking around ideas for such an airplane for years. Back in the 1940s when he was plotting out his first three projects and boldly allocating "HT" designations, the HT-3 was envisioned as a simple one- or two-seater. At the time the idea had progressed no further than a few sketches variously labeled "HXT-3" and "XHT-3 Sport Plane."

But in 1960 when he started the Aero Wing project, he formally assigned the HT-3 designation to it. Then in the 1970s, when it appeared his new sport plane would fly before the Aero Wing, the issue became further confused. He switched the designation back again, filing an affidavit of ownership for the sport plane as the HT-3. Presumably the Aero Wing would then become the HT-4, but it was never denoted as such. In reality these numeric designations meant little to Bruce, and beyond his youthful musings, he only used them on legal paperwork submitted to the FAA. In normal conversation, he referred to his creations by their common names.

Bruce's sport plane kit would be a fun side-by-side two-seater, something sleek and different that a builder could be proud of and that anyone would love to own. It would not be the simplest of kit planes, but a project for the ambitious and experienced builder. A 150-hp engine would be buried inside the fuselage behind the cabin. The rear-mounted power plant would actually face forward and drive the two pusher propellers through a system of internal V-belts. The design featured gull wings — the short inboard sections sweeping forward and upward, the main outboard sections sweeping back. Prop shafts protruded rearward from the wing bends.

The jaunty gull wings lent a distinctly avian look, and Bruce dubbed his design the Pterodactyl, after the prehistoric flying reptile. Through the decades, that ancient creature's name seems to have sounded just the right note of awe and wonder for more than one designer of tailless airplanes. Most notably the British Westland-Hill designs of the 1920s and 30s had appropriated the evocative moniker. And more recently an ultralight has been marketed as

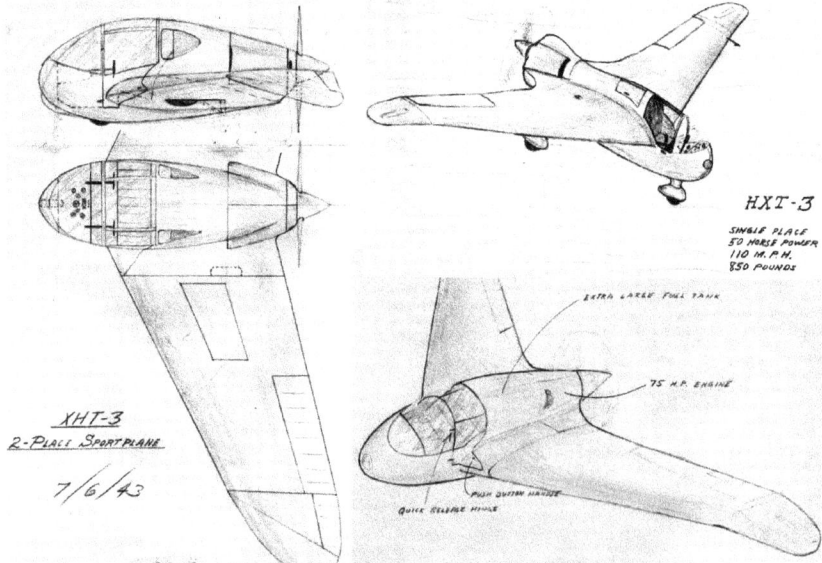

Sport plane ideas sketched by Bruce K. Hallock in the 1940s.

a Pterodactyl. At the time, though, Bruce considered the name uncommon enough, and he stuck with it.

Although the gull wings and twin-propeller arrangement were the most striking features of the Hallock Pterodactyl, the most un-

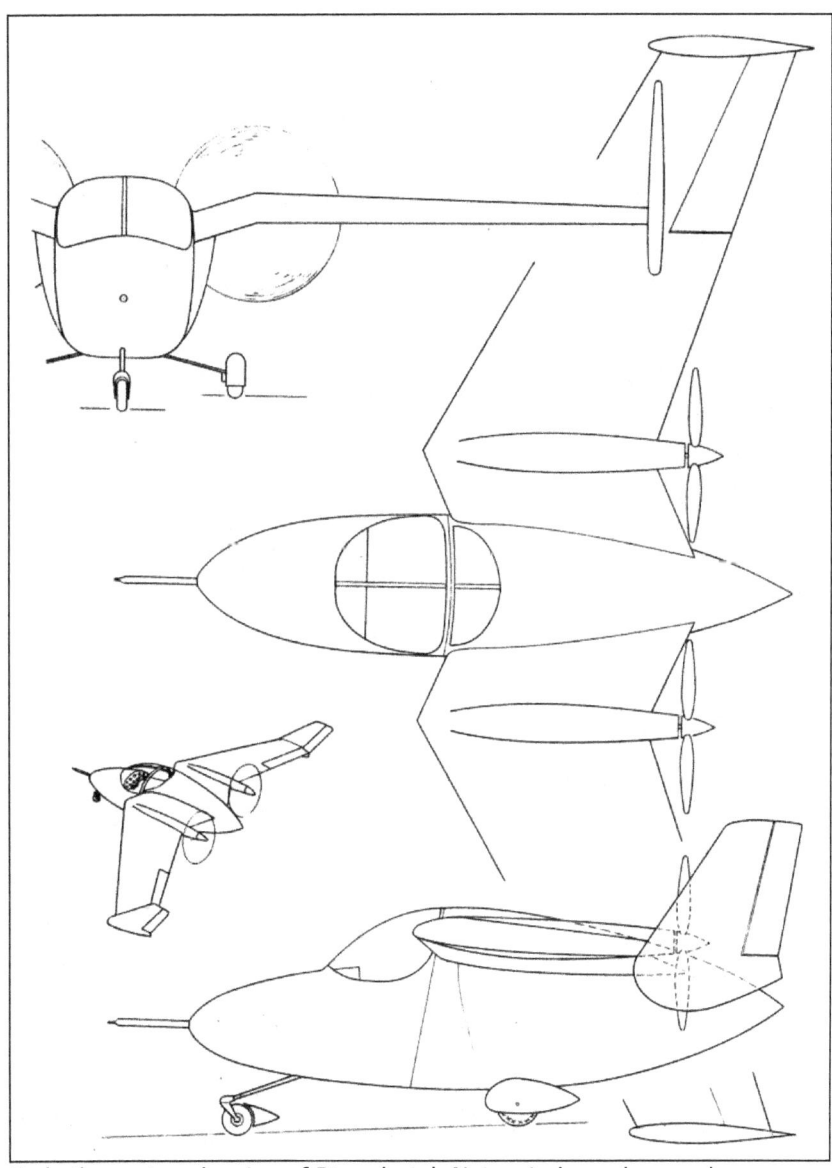

Early three-view drawing of Pterodactyl. Note windows shown where escape hatch was eventually installed. Also note engine air scoops shown in front view.

usual was probably the means of entry. The entire nose shell, all the way back to mid-cabin (including the windshield), slid forward on tracks mounted beneath the cabin floor. The floor stayed put, so the pilot and passenger stepped in and out on either side without having to clamber, scrunch, or duck. In the event of a mishap's preventing the nose section from sliding open, an escape hatch located behind and above the seats could be used.

In 1973 Bruce pushed the unfinished Aero Wing fuselage into the corner of his North Austin workshop and began construction of the Pterodactyl. The question arises: Was the Pterodactyl a distraction from the all-important Aero Wing project, which he had vowed to follow through? The answer must be both yes and no. The Pterodactyl came along at a time when the prospects for obtaining financial backing for the Aero Wing had dried up. Although Bruce had been proceeding with the Aero Wing project using his own limited funds, he was still casting about for other sources of capital. He wanted the sales of Pterodactyl kits and plans to help finance and promote the Aero Wing — in hindsight a tenuous proposition indeed.

But the need to raise capital was only one reason for switching ventures in midcourse. The Pterodactyl project would allow him to acquire firsthand knowledge of new materials and construction techniques that would be directly applicable to the Aero Wing. And he would gain insights that would help him further refine the Aero Wing's design. In this way the Pterodactyl would serve as a sort of laboratory for the larger project. But the ultimate reason for diverting his efforts was probably more subjective. Although he may not have admitted it, the idea of the Pterodactyl caught his fancy at a time when his larger project had bogged down. His colleagues were building and flying their own sport planes, and he yearned to be part of that excitement. In that sense the Pterodactyl was really a bit of a lark.

* * *

Bruce wanted to finish the Pterodactyl quickly and start showing it off at fly-ins. He drew up three-views and sketched out some of the essentials, but many elements he designed as he built. He hired an assistant, John Langston, a skilled aircraft mechanic and resourceful worker who also became a good friend. Bruce salvaged a 150-hp Lycoming O-320 from a wrecked Piper Cherokee 140, and John rebuilt the engine.

When John started on the project, Bruce was already well along with the fuselage. As he progressed, Bruce mocked up major components with plywood and cardboard before committing to the final form. The basic frame was bolted I-beam and channel aluminum with some tubular steel in the engine mount. The cabin floor and the front and rear bulkheads were plywood, but other formers and the rest of the fuselage structure were sheet aluminum. Most of the exterior skin was also aluminum, but certain prominent contours were foam or fiberglass or both. The nose was molded as a single piece of fiberglass. On the tailpiece, foam was used to fill in the voids and fiberglass cloth was applied on top. Through his work on the Motor Rickshaw, Bruce had attained extensive skill in working with fiberglass. And this knack for shaping molds and forms extended all the way back to his model-airplane days when he had become an ace at sculpting balsawood and carving propellers.

In the transition from plans to reality, the project underwent only one major design change. Early drawings and notes show that Bruce intended to incorporate retracting nose-mounted canard wings similar to those he was designing for the Aero Wing. But as the project developed, this idea was abandoned—probably in an effort to avoid complexity.

The Pterodactyl used only a few hardware items salvaged from other airplanes. The main landing gear came from a Cessna 150. The nose gear and full-swivel nose wheel had been the tail-wheel assembly of a Cessna 180. The airplane would be steered by the main wheel brakes.

The propeller-shaft housings were fabricated of common four-inch, schedule-40 PVC pipe. The material was cheap, but also light and strong. The wing spars, ribs, and coverings were of conventional aluminum construction—likewise the vertical fins. However, the wing leading edges and vertical-fin tips were foam. For the control surfaces, Bruce opted for an even more adventurous approach. He and John cut the rib forms from half-inch slabs of a rigid, PVC-based, closed-cell foam. The foam ribs were then epoxied to the thin aluminum skins of the elevons and rudders. This construction method, which had been tested and proven in sailplanes, provided very light yet rigid structures.

Despite the use of certain lightweight materials, it became apparent that the emergent airframe had a weight problem. The spring steel main gear started to splay outward, and the Pterodactyl's belly hung low. John Langston pointed out that prototypes are frequently heaver than anticipated. Still confident that weight could be trimmed from later versions, Bruce installed a skid at the rear of the fuselage to guard against scraping bottom on test flights.

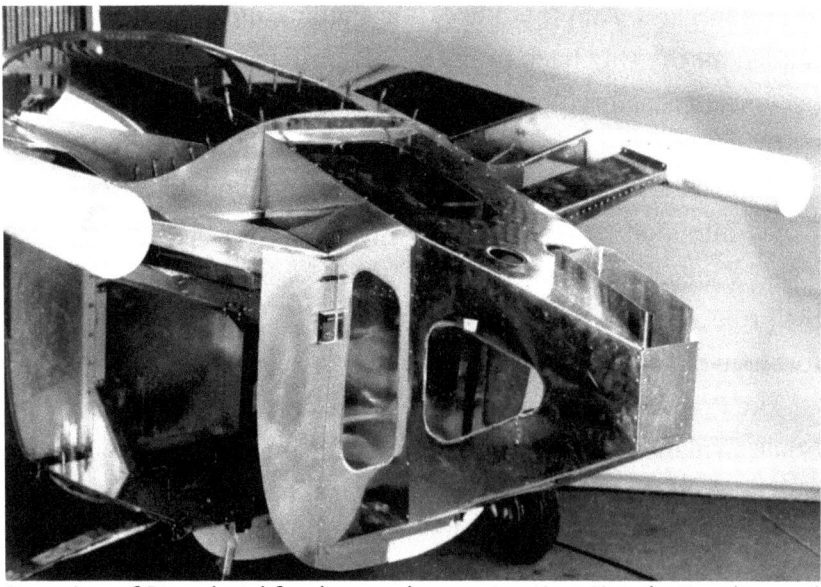

Rear view of Pterodactyl fuselage under construction. Note battery box and PVC-pipe propeller shaft housings.

For initial runway testing, Bruce wanted to tow the unpowered Pterodactyl behind an automobile. For this purpose he installed two tow hooks at the wing bends right under the leading edges. Towing would allow the airplane to become briefly airborne—just long enough to test the effectiveness of the control surfaces. He would then release the tow cables, and the plane would settle back down on the runway.

B. K. Hallock and partially finished Pterodactyl fuselage. Nose is mocked up at this point.

Pterodactyl wings under construction.

John Langston working on the Pterodactyl's engine compartment.

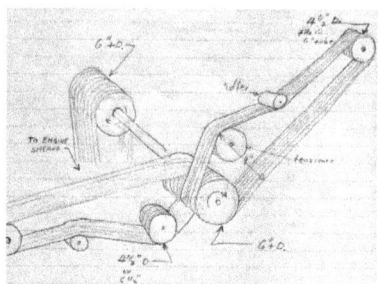
Early conceptual sketch of the Pterodactyl's belt-drive system.

* * *

As it neared completion, the Pterodactyl generated considerable excitement among local EAA members. Bruce didn't really want to create a big stir before the project was finished, but the news got around. Enthusiasts dropped by, and it didn't take much coaxing to get him to show and explain the airplane's fine points. In 1974 he exhibited the half-finished airframe at a regional fly-in, taking first prize in the "static display" category. In 1977 a local paper ran a story with photos of the nearly complete pterodactyl. And famed designer Burt Rutan even came by to have a look when he was in town conducting a seminar on composite construction techniques.

Unfinished Pterodactyl with engine installed on display at fly-in in Kerrville, Texas, 1974. Pictured from left to right: Dr. Ron Stearman, John Langston, unknown person in background, Luke Null, Bruce K. Hallock, and Tony Bingelis (in front of Bruce).

The Pterodactyl got a striking white paint job with light blue accent striping. It looked finished, but one major item remained incomplete—the system for transmitting power to the propellers. For this Bruce planned to use an elaborate array of V-belts. Walter Birtchfield, an EAA colleague, custom machined a large eight-groove sheave from solid aluminum. This sheave was attached directly to the engine output shaft. Eight belts would connect it to a jackshaft mounted directly above the engine. The jackshaft would turn a 16-groove sheave, which distributed power to the propellers —eight belts to each side, all concealed within the wing roots.

The two sheaves for the jackshaft were also custom machined. To help dampen torque loads during engine starts, acceleration, and deceleration, Bruce planned to install a Flexidyne dry-fluid coupling on the jackshaft. The coupling was purchased but never installed.

In fact the propeller-drive system was never completed. By 1979 Bruce had halted work on the Pterodactyl. To the casual observer, this turn of events was baffling. The airplane was nearly finished— why didn't he go ahead and get it in the air? Bruce was cagey about his rationale, perhaps a bit embarrassed that he had expended so much money and effort only to abandon the project. Eventually several explanations emerged, which considered together, probably add up to some kind of justification.

The airframe was overweight, and it became obvious that the 150-hp Lycoming would not provide adequate power. In addition, Bruce estimated that the friction inherent in the belt-drive system would rob about ten percent of the available power. But if it were simply a question of power, a larger engine should have solved the problem—or a second, lighter prototype. Other factors undoubtedly contributed to the termination.

Between its inception and the time Bruce's project neared completion, the world of kit airplanes had seen tremendous advances. A profusion of new designs and construction techniques had become available, and many of them made the Pterodactyl seem ill-suited to the current market. The trend was toward composite materials and simple, easy-to-build designs. Aluminum was relatively heavy and expensive, and working with it required a degree of expertise that most kit builders did not possess. Furthermore, Bruce realized that the mechanics, especially the belt-driven propellers, were overly complex. In a moment of candor, he admitted, "I have a tendency to envision things that are too complicated — even the Motor Rickshaw." Then he added, "I don't like to follow trends, so consequently it gets too complicated."

Whatever his reasons, Bruce's attention had turned to other matters. At the end of the 1970s, he and Enid and their son Gary embarked on the construction of a fifteen-unit apartment complex. Alongside the apartments Bruce built a larger workshop (2,300 square feet) and resumed work on the Aero Wing. The Pterodactyl was moved into a corner of the shop where it gathered dust over the ensuing decades and piqued the curiosity of visitors.

Although the Pterodactyl never flew, the effort expended on it yielded some rewards. The project allowed Bruce to hone his skill at working with aluminum. He also acquired valuable experience in the use of fiberglass, plastics, and other new materials. And perhaps most significantly, he gained practical insights into certain structural challenges directly applicable to the Aero Wing. His decision to move the Aero Wing's vertical fins from the wingtips to the wing pods (closer to the wing root) resulted from his experience with the Pterodactyl, whose wingtip-mounted rudders had necessitated significant additional reinforcement of the cantilever wings.

The unfinished Pterodactyl continued to play an instructive role in other ways. Its impeccable workmanship set the benchmark for the many aspiring airplane builders who visited Bruce's workshop. Other would-be designers drew inspiration from its sleek lines and novel features. And in his moments of brooding reflection, Bruce himself may have looked over at the spry little airplane — perched high on 55-gallon drums to keep it safely out of the way — and found encouragement to carry on.

Bruce demonstrates the Pterodactyl's sliding nose section.

Bruce K. Hallock and his 95%-finished Pterodactyl, Austin, Texas, circa 1976.

Pterodactyl glamour shot.

* * *

While working on the Pterodactyl during the 1970s, Bruce's association with the local EAA chapter remained especially strong. As president he became intimately involved with the monthly meetings, and he took a personal interest in other members' projects. Jim Newman, an old friend from the days of Austin Aero Service, was also a member of the club and a devoted amateur builder. His project at the time was a Smith Mini-Plane, a small single-seat biplane popular among EAA members. After several years of work, Jim finally had the airplane ready to fly. He'd scratch-built it from plans, and the little bright-orange beauty reflected the care and time lavished on it.

Jim considered Bruce a thorough and careful pilot and asked him to test fly the new plane. Bruce accepted and, on the appointed date, appeared at Tim's Airpark, a sizable uncontrolled airport north of Austin that served as EAA Chapter 187's home base in those days. A crowd gathered around the Mini-Plane. Pictures were taken as Bruce conducted his final inspection.

Jim had constructed the airplane according to the plans — with one exception. Instead of the standard double-strut landing gear, he had used a modified single-leg design. Bruce expressed confidence in Jim's workmanship and, with flying helmet and goggles in place, climbed into the cockpit.

Several times he raced the Mini-Plane down the runway to get a feel for the controls and assure himself that the craft was sound. All seemed well; so on the next run, he lifted off briefly and immediately set the plane back down.

When the full weight of the plane came down on the modified landing gears, something twisted, and the wheels started tracking in different directions. As Bruce struggled to hold the plane on a straight course, both gears suddenly collapsed. The biplane thumped onto its belly, skidded off the runway, and whipped around backwards.

Bruce wasn't hurt, just embarrassed for having "bent" someone else's airplane in front of the whole club. The fault, however, was later found to be with the modified landing gear. Since only the propeller and landing gear had suffered in the mishap, Jim was able to reconstruct the gear according to the original plans and get the Mini-Plane ready to fly again. Afterwards it handled very nicely.

Jim Newman later sold the plane to another EAA member, Cody Godwin, who fared less well with it. One evening while hedgehopping in the Mini-Plane, Cody flew into some telephone wires and crashed in a field. His neck snapped, and he died instantly.

* * *

By the end of the 1970s, Bruce began to derive more of his income from sources other than aviation, namely investment and real estate. But his professional flying and consulting continued intermittently through the 1980s and into the 1990s.

One of his more interesting undertakings involved Dr. Ron Stearman, professor of aerospace engineering and engineering mechanics at the University of Texas at Austin. Stearman was — and still is — a recognized authority on thin-shell monocoque construction and on flutter and vibration, among other things. He also happened to be a first cousin once removed of Lloyd Stearman of the Kydet biplane fame. He and Bruce met through the EAA in the mid 1970s.

Dr. Stearman was not directly associated with the University's Applied Research Laboratories, but he did have some University-sponsored aviation projects of his own. One centered on an obscure airplane called the Windecker Eagle. From a distance the Eagle didn't appear particularly distinctive. In general outline, it could have been the second cousin of a Mooney 201 or Beechcraft Bonanza—just another modern-day, four-place, single-engine, low-wing monoplane with retractable landing gear. But structurally the Windecker Eagle was completely different. The airframe was constructed entirely of composite material, and it was the first such aircraft to attain FAA certification.

A total of nine Eagle airplanes had been built in Midland, Texas. Two of that number were prototype test aircraft. The first prototype had crashed during certification testing. In early 1980 Ron Stearman managed to have the second prototype donated to the University of Texas Aerospace Engineering Department with the intention of setting up a student flight-test program.

Since Bruce was already known at the University as a talented and safe pilot, Dr. Stearman enlisted him as pilot and caretaker for the Eagle. Bruce was asked to fly the airplane on a regular basis to keep its status current. He flew Dr. Stearman on several trips in the Eagle, most notably to a composite aircraft workshop sponsored by the NASA Langley Research Center in Newport News, Virginia. The Eagle was on display there for about a week while the two men attended technical meetings. Bruce also gave a couple of NASA test pilots check rides in the airplane.

The light-blue Eagle was housed in the same hangar with the Lab's DC-3. Bruce remembered that at least once the professor brought some of his students out to the airport; they attached eccentric spinning weights to various parts of the airplane's control surfaces and measured the vibrations with an oscillograph as part of a class project. But Mother Nature soon dashed all hope of using the Eagle in a full-fledged student flight-test program. Less than a year after the airplane was acquired by the University, a tornado tore through Austin's Robert Mueller Airport, wrecking many of the aircraft based on the north side of the field. By this time the DC-3 had been sold off, but the Windecker was totally destroyed. Parts of it were found out between the runways and several blocks into the surrounding neighborhood.

* * *

Although Bruce's professional flying tapered off in the mid 1980s, his personal flying continued unabated. Until the fateful tornado that descended on Robert Mueller Airport in 1980, his Navion had shared hangar space with the University's Windecker Eagle. Both Bruce and his airplane happened to be out of town at the time of the storm. Afterwards he moved the Navion to Kitty Hill, a two-runway, grass-strip airfield north of Austin.

Other EAA members were also beginning to base their planes at Kitty Hill. The little airport was privately owned and operated by Bill and Kitty Huggins, who lived on the property. Numerous hangars were being erected there, and Bruce and sons built their own. The developing community of light-plane enthusiasts sponsored several fly-ins and picnics at the site. On a couple of these occasions, Bruce watched in delight as a radio-controlled replica of his prize-winning 1939 Bobtail looped and soared overhead. Local aero-modeler John Dana had reproduced the distinctive tailless from the original plans.

Navion N5202K continued to put in appearances at fly-ins around the country until about 1988, when Bruce dismantled the airplane in anticipation of a complete overhaul. The project then vied for attention with other ongoing ventures and was never completed. Even without the Navion, he continued to attend fly-ins. Sometimes he flew with friends, and sometimes he drove. Always he camped out. He liked to travel, and he remained an enthusiastic student of new developments in aviation and related technologies.

As a leader in his field, Bruce eagerly helped and encouraged a new generation of aviation enthusiasts. Charles Yant and John Langston have already been mentioned, but there was a host of others, including his son Don, who became an avid pilot and airplane owner under his father's tutelage.

Jay Miller was a fresh college graduate and curator of the University of Texas's aviation collection in the early 1970s. His interest in unusual aircraft led him to photograph the Applied Research Labs' TC-47K (DC-3). In the process Jay happened upon the full-scale mockup of Bruce's Aero Wing, which at the time, occupied a corner of the University's hangar at Robert Mueller Municipal Airport. Shortly thereafter Jay met Bruce at an EAA meeting, and their mutual interest in exotic aircraft drew them into a close friendship. Jay wasn't a pilot, but he was eager to fly, and he traveled with Bruce to many fly-ins. "I had a lot of faith in his skills as a pilot and his knowledge of the hardware," said Jay. "He wasn't one to leave much to chance, and I liked that." This sentiment was echoed by many passengers and other pilots who flew with Bruce over the years.

Jay enjoyed wowing Bruce with esoteric tidbits of aviation history. "His response was always genuine and always appropriate," said Jay. "I can still hear him say 'Golly' or 'Gosh' or 'Gee Whiz'— which, coming from any other person, would have been a backhanded insult—but from him, it was the highest praise." The two men remained close friends as Jay went on to become an internationally renowned aviation photographer, historian, author, and publisher.

Peter Coltman, a young friend of the Hallock family with a precocious interest in flying, often plied Bruce for advice and guidance. He eventually moved into a career as a pilot for American Airlines. Peter also maintained a couple of planes of his own. He and Bruce remained close for many years, flying and working on their airplanes together.

Carl Vernon was another of the younger generation of fliers who befriended Bruce, much to the mutual benefit of both men. After learning to fly, Carl began avidly buying and selling airplanes. He and Bruce partnered to rebuild and sell a couple of Cessnas. Eventually Bruce extended a loan to help Carl open a flying service at nearby Lago Vista Airport. In a sense, this endeavor had brought him full circle; Bruce was helping to propagate the kind of business that had launched his own civil aviation career back in the 1940s.

And there were many others. A continual procession of EAA buddies and other enthusiasts came by Bruce's shop seeking help and advice. He never seemed to resent these intrusions; in fact he went out of his way to share his arsenal of specialized tools and his wide-ranging expertise. One EAA friend who lacked workspace of his own constructed an entire airplane in Bruce's shop.

If he knew his time was running out, Bruce never acted like it. He just kept methodically working on his Aero Wing as circumstances permitted. Grandchildren arrived. Apartments needed tending. Myriad other interests and obligations pressed in. And all these diversions, from the sublime to the mundane, tore away the calendar pages.

By the turn of the century, Bruce's piloting days had ended. With over 14,000 hours in the cockpit, his memories were many. But his thoughts were more often on the future than the past. He maintained a keen interest in his own projects and those of his friends. And the sound of an engine overhead never failed to stir his imagination.

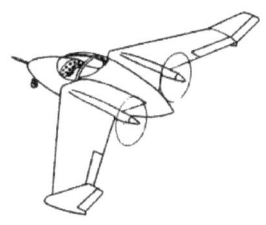

Epilogue

Throughout most of his life, Bruce K. Hallock had been a model of health and vigor. So in 2004 when he began to lose strength in one arm, everyone assumed he would just overcome the problem through his usual regimen of exercise and clean living. But this was to be a different sort of challenge. In the spring of 2005, Bruce was diagnosed with amyotrophic lateral sclerosis — ALS — also known as Lou Gehrig's disease. It's a degenerative neurological disease marked by progressive muscle weakness and atrophy. And ultimately ALS is fatal. Despite the gloomy prognosis and his deteriorating condition, Bruce maintained an affable demeanor. ALS does not affect the mind, and he remained sharp-witted and engaging to the end.

Most of the interviews that formed the basis of this book were conducted in Bruce's last year. He died at home on the last day of November 2005.

The family held a memorial service at a church across the street from Austin's old Robert Mueller Municipal Airport, from whose runways Bruce had taken off on so many journeys. He probably would have preferred a formation flyby of Pterodactyls and Aero Wings, but the profusion of remembrances and heartfelt tributes was more than most men could hope for. Bruce's legacy was large. Beyond the airplanes and vehicles and buildings, he left behind an extended family and network of friends who remained indebted to him for years of support, guidance, and companionship.

In 2006 the Frontiers of Flight Museum, located at Love Field in Dallas, acquired Bruce's Road Wing and Pterodactyl. The two airplanes are currently being restored for display at the museum. The unfinished Aero Wing fuselage is on display at the Hidden Hangar, a civil-aviation museum run by Bruce's son Don Hallock in Truth or Consequences, New Mexico.

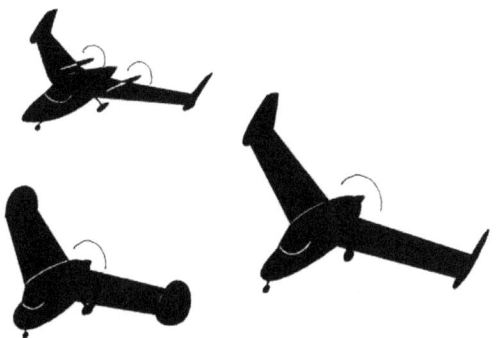

INDEX

Individual models of airplanes, vehicles, and engines are listed under their respective manufacturers — except for those of Bruce K. Hallock, each of which has a separate entry.

Entries for some persons include a parenthetical note indicating their relationship to Bruce K. Hallock (BKH), for example, (boyhood friend), (flight instructor), (wife), etc.

Academy of Model Aeronautics, 8
aerial photography, 151
Aero Commander, 167–168
Aero King. *See* Aero Wing
Aero Wing (other names: HT-3, Aero King):
    artist's conception, 173, 175
    concept and original design, 159–164
    construction, 162, 168, 174, 204, 210, 217
    design changes, 167–169, 170–173, 210
    end of project, 174–176, 217
    engine for, 169–170
    final disposition of, 219
    financing of, 164-167, 198, 204
    marketing of, 159–160, 163–164, 194–195
    naming and designation of, 160, 201
    static display model, 161, 168, 170
    test model, 170, 171
    mentioned, 177, 205, 216, 218
aerobatics, 31, 34, 35, 61, 180
Aerobella. *See* Aeronca Chief
Aeronca aircraft:
    Champion, 78–79, 82, 84, 85, 86
    Chief, 52, 55, 56–60, 63–66, 75
    Sedan, 87, 95–96, 99, 105
Aerosphere, 157
Air Force, U. S. (Army), 22, 36, 29, 41, 63, 82, 84, 100, 150
Air Trails magazine, 10
air-combat maneuvering range, 186
airships, 5–8
airworthiness, 62, 199
Akron Road (in Medina, Ohio), 14, 65

Akron, Ohio, 5, 10, 13, 15, 17, 20
Akron, USS (the airship), 5–8
Alliance, Ohio, 18, 79
Allison engine, 169
Allred, James, 123–124
American Airlines, 144, 145, 147, 148, 216
American Modelers Association, 8
amyotrophic lateral sclerosis (ALS), 218
Andes Mountains:
    flying over, 114–116, 119
    traversing by train & bus, 117–118, 139
Andros Island, Bahamas, 50
Applied Physics Laboratory, Johns Hopkins University, 178
Applied Research Laboratories (ARL), 181–193, 198, 214, 216. *See also* Defense Research Laboratory
AR-15 automatic rifle, 189
Army Air Force. *See* Air Force
Army, U. S., 38
Aruba, 186–190, 192
Atlanta, Georgia, 42, 79
atomic bomb, 63
Atwood Phantom model engine, 16
Augusta, Georgia, 63
Austin Aero Service, 82–88, 93, 97, 98, 212. *See also* St. Edward's Airport
Austin, Texas, 38–40, 42, 53, 82–87, 93, 95, 96, 97, 98, 100, 101, 102, 103, 104, 105, 106, 110, 111, 114, 115, 122, 124, 125, 128, 129, 130, 135, 138, 139, 142, 143, 145, 148, 149, 152,

221

Austin, Texas (continued), 155, 177, 182, 183, 186, 189, 191, 193, 198, 200, 204, 211, 212, 213, 215, 218
auto rickshaw, 154. *See also* Motor Rickshaw

Baffle Bird:
    early name for Road Wing, 89. (*See also* Road Wing)
    large flying model that prefigured the Road Wing, 23–24, 27–28, 75, 89
Bahamas, 50
Bales, Bill, 152–153
ball lightning, 50
Balsa Butchers, 18, 20
Barony chair, 30, 32
Baxter, John (Navy colleague), 69
BD-5, 201
Beaumont, Texas, 151
Beckner, Fred, 178, 180, 187, 188, 189
Bede, Jim, 201
Beech aircraft:
    AT-11 Kansan, 41
    AT-7 Navigator, 41
    Bonanza, 143, 145, 160, 192, 196, 214
    C-45, 37
    Model 18 (variously known as Twin Beech, C-45, & SNB), 37, 41–42, 125, 126, 142, 143, 145, 147–150, 152, 177–180, 184
    SNB, 41–42, 177
Beeville, Texas, 37, 38, 40
Belém, Brazil, 45
Belize City, British Honduras, 98–99, 101–102, 103, 111
Bellanca Cruisemaster, 160
Bendix Trophy, 11
Bennett, Floyd, Sr., 10, 14
Bennett, Jack (boyhood friend), 9
Bergstrom Air Force Base, 39, 84
Beta Theta Pi Fraternity, 17
Beveridge, Bert, 126, 127, 128, 129, 130, 139, 141, 145, 152, 165, 166, 199
Biloxi, Mississippi, 59, 61
Bingelis, Tony, 200, 208
Birchfield, Walter, 192
Bishop Airport (Flint, Michigan), 130, 133, 134

Bobtail (flying model), 14–17, 18, 215
Boeing aircraft:
    B-17 Flying Fortress, 25, 36, 73
    Model 727, 192
Boise, Idaho, 31, 32, 33, 40
Borman, Bub, 110, 111
boxing the station, 48
Brazil, 45
Brian Memorial Methodist Church (Miami, Florida), 53
British Honduras (Belize), 98–99, 101–102, 103, 104, 111
Bromberg Special, 12
Brown Junior model engine, 10
Browning Aerial Service (Austin, Texas), 101, 125
Brownsville, Texas, 95, 96, 97, 100, 103, 111, 123, 125
Bullock, Bob, 150
Bullpup missile, 184–185
Bump, Leona (flight instructor), 31–32, 33
Burgess-Dunne airplanes, 19
Burke Lakefront Airport (Cleveland, Ohio), 141
Bush, George H. W., 59

Cali, Colombia, 114–116
Campeche, Bay of, 101
Campeche, Mexico, 103
Canal Zone, Panama, 113, 141
canard-type aircraft, 201
canard wing, 171–172, 205
Caravan (Hallock HT-2), 158–159
Caribbean Sea, 45, 62, 68, 98, 186, 188
Case Institute of Technology (and Case Western Reserve University), 10, 14, 18–20
Cebu, Philippines, 68
Cerro de Pasco, Peru, 118
certification (CAA and FAA), 91, 165, 166, 167, 198, 199, 214
Cessna aircraft:
    Model 150, 205
    Model 180, 205
    Model 208 Caravan, 158
    Model 210, 160
    UC-78 Bobcat, 87–88, 94
Chance Vought aircraft:
    F4U Corsair, 121, 190
    F7U Cutlass, 120–121

Chance Vought Corporation, 120–122, 125
Chevrolet engine, 169
Chicago, Illinois, 79, 127, 128
Civil Aeronautics Administration (CAA), 91. *See also* Federal Aviation Administration
Civilian Pilot Training Program, 29
Cleco fastener, 20
Cleveland Air Races. *See* National Air Races
Cleveland Graphite Bronze, 21
Cleveland Pneumatic Tool Company, 20, 27
Cleveland Press, 17
Cleveland, Ohio, 10, 11, 14, 17, 18, 20, 21, 22, 40, 65, 90, 91, 141
Cloer, Ted, 177–178, 179, 180, 181, 182–183, 184–185, 186, 187, 189, 190, 191–192
Coast Guard, U. S., 44
Coco Solo Naval Air Station, Panama, 46, 62
Coconut Grove (Miami, Florida), 53
Colombia, 113–116, 141
Coltman, Peter, 216
Columbia, South Carolina, 63, 65
Condron Field, New Mexico, 180
Connally, John, 143
Consolidated B-24 Liberator, 73
Consolidated Vultee, 91
Continental engines:
    220-hp radial, 35
    65-hp, 58
    0-300, 96, 105, 106
Convair aircraft:
    B-36 Peacemaker, 26
    ConVairCar, 91–92
    Model 240, 144, 150
composite materials, 208, 210, 214. *See also* fiberglass
Corpus Christi, Texas, 38, 41, 42, 87
Costa Rica, 112, 140, 141
Cronkite, Walter, 143
crop dusting, 106–109
Cuba, 45
Culver PQ-14 Cadet, 70–71
Curtiss (and Curtiss-Wright) aircraft:
    C-46 Commando, 187–188
    F9C Sparrowhawk, 7
    JN-4 Jenny, 1, 2, 5
    Pursuit (model of), 8
    SB2C Helldiver, 26

Curtiss electric propeller, 45
Curtiss-Wright Field (Milwaukee, Wisconsin), 199
Customs Service, U. S., 96–97, 103

Dallas Aero (Dallas, Texas), 130
Dallas Executive Airport, 121
Dallas, Texas, 100, 104, 120, 121, 126, 130, 145, 218
Damn Good Airplane (DGA), 11
Dana, John, 215
Darién, Panama, 113, 141
David, Panama, 112
Davis, Buster, 86, 87
Dayton, Ohio, 22, 24, 40, 43
D-Day, 42
de Havilland 104 Dove, 126–130, 131, 139, 141, 151, 199
Declaration of Temporary Sojourn, 111, 122
Defense Research Laboratory (DRL), 177–181. *See also* Applied Research Laboratories
Delray Beach, Florida, 127, 128
Detroit, Michigan, 129, 141
Dinner Key (Miami, Florida), 44, 45, 46–47, 48, 49, 53, 55, 60
dirigible. *See* airship
Dominican Republic, 45
Douglas aircraft:
    C-47 Skytrain, 27
    DC-3 (variously known as C-47, R4D, & TC-47K), 27, 43, 61, 119, 125, 144, 181–193, 214, 215, 216
    DC-4, 119
    R4D, 61, 62, 67, 69
    TC-47K (also called DC-3), 181, 186, 216
    XB-19, 26
    mentioned, 103
Driskill Hotel (Austin, Texas), 38

Ecuador, 116
Effinger, Robert (Bob) (boyhood friend), 9, 10
Eisenhower, Dwight David, 42, 142
El Paso, Texas, 191–192
Eldred, Dewey, 21
elevons, 133, 173, 206
Ellston, Stu, 132
Ercoupe, 94

experimental aircraft:
   Aero Wing as, 153, 169, 175
   definition of, 199
   military, 23, 25, 26, 120
   Road Wing as, 134, 137.
   See also homebuilt aircraft
Experimental Aircraft Association
   (EAA):
   Chapter 187, 200, 212
   inception and purpose of, 199–200
   involvement with, 199–201, 208,
      209, 212–213, 215, 216, 217

Fair Oil Company, 125–126
Fair, Ralph E., 125
Fairchild PT-19, 87
Fauvel, Charles, 19
Fawcett Airlines, 119
Federal Aviation Administration (FAA),
   133–134, 141, 165, 166, 167,
   181, 186, 193, 198, 199, 202,
   214. *See also* Civil Aeronautics
   Administration
fiberglass:
   use in homebuilt aircraft, 201
   use in Motor Rickshaw, 154, 155
   use in Pterodactyl, 205, 210
   use on TC-47K, 182, 184, 185.
   See also composite materials
fire engine. *See* Hallock Chemical
   Truck
flight instructor's rating, 80
Flint, Michigan, 126, 130, 135, 165
Floating Feather Airport (Boise,
   Idaho), 31–32
Floresville, Texas, 103
flying boats, 44–51, 61–62, 73
Flying magazine, 8
Ford Model T, 14
Fort Lauderdale, Florida, 56, 193
Fortaleza, Brazil, 45
Fowler flaps, 170, 171
Franklin engines, 70, 91
Frontiers of Flight Museum, 218
Fulton Airphibian, 90, 91
Fulton, Robert, 91

Ganyard, Floyd (boyhood friend), 9
Garner, John Nance, 143–144
gascolator, 64
General Land Office, Texas, 150–152,
   153
General Motors TBM Avenger, 59, 60

Gensemer, Wade (boyhood friend), 9
Georgetown, British Guyana, 45
GI Bill of Rights (Servicemen's
   Readjustment Act of 1944), 80,
   83, 97, 121
Godwin, Cody, 213
golf carts, 152–153, 155
Goodyear-Zeppelin Co., 5
gosport, 34
Grand Prairie, Texas, 120–121
Granville Brothers Gee Bee racers, 11
Great War, the *See* World War I
Groton, Connecticut, 179
Grumman aircraft:
   F4F Wildcat, 59–60
   F6F Hellcat, 69–70, 71, 190
   F8F Bearcat, 190
   F9F, 177
   TBF Avenger, (*See* General Motors
      TBM Avenger)
Guantanamo, Cuba, 45
Guatemala, 95, 98, 188, 189–190
Guatemala City, Guatemala, 189–190
Guayaquil, Gulf of, 116
Gunter Hotel (San Antonio, Texas),
   103
Gypsy Queen engine, 126

Haigler, Albert Dale (Methodist
   pastor), 53
Haile Airport (Austin, Texas), 101
Haiti, 45
Hall, Stan, 22
Hall, Theodore P., 91
Hallock, Bruce Glen (first son), 83, 99,
   109, 110, 156, 139, 197
Hallock, Bruce King:
   birth, 6
   book on tailless aircraft design, 23,
      76–78
   childhood, 1–3, 5–13
   college, 14, 17–20
   design philosophy, 18–19, 89–93,
      159–164
   death, 174, 218
   engagement to Enid, 42, 52
   first airplane ride, 13
   flight instructor, 80, 82
   flight training, advanced, 34–38,
      40–43, 69, 121
   flight training, beginning, 21, 31–
      32
   marriage to Enid, 51, 52–54

Hallock, Bruce King (continued):
military service, 29–74
Hallock Chemical Truck (fire engine),
14–15
Hallock, Clara Louise (sister), 6, 9
Hallock, Clara (née Ulmer) (mother),
6, 7, 9, 14
Hallock, Don or Donald Macy (second
son), 83, 110, 134, 139, 156,
173, 175, 193, 197, 216, 219
Hallock, Enid (née MacPherson)
(wife):
engagement to BKH, 42
marriage to BKH, 52–54
meeting BKH, 38–40
solo flight and piloting, 84–85
mentioned, 23, 43, 51, 55–59, 63–
66, 68, 73, 78–79, 82, 83, 84,
85, 93, 99, 100, 101, 105, 109,
110, 111–119, 121, 122, 123,
130, 134, 135, 139–140, 145,
156, 157, 185–186, 191, 194,
195, 197
Hallock, Gary Mac (third son), 121,
134, 139, 156, 168, 197, 210
Hallock, Helen (sister), 6, 9
Hallock, Macy Monroe (brother), 5, 6,
9, 11, 14, 59–61
Hallock, Macy Orsen (father), 1–2, 5,
6, 9, 10, 11, 13, 14, 15, 19, 20,
22, 65, 80
Hallock, Mark Stephen (fourth son),
128, 134, 139, 156, 197
Hallock, Thomas (Tom) (uncle), 14,
15
Hallock Tailless aircraft designations,
general discussion of, 75–76,
200–201. *See also* Road Wing,
HT-2, *and* HT-3.
Hidden Hangar Museum (Truth or
Consequences, New Mexico),
219
Hiroshima, Japan, 63
Hockaday, Lt. (Navy flight instructor),
34
Hoff, Matt (Naval-cadet cohort), 35–
36
Hoffa, James P. (Jimmy), 129
homebuilt aircraft, 134, 199, 200,
201. *See also* experimental
aircraft
Honduras, 112
Honduras, Gulf of, 111

Honolulu, Hawaii, 67
Hopkins Field (Cleveland, Ohio), 10
Houston, Texas, 104, 125
Howard, Ben, 11
HT-1 (Hallock Tailless #1). *See* Road
Wing
HT-2 (Hallock Tailless #2):
early concept, 75, 77. (*See also*
Caravan)
later concept (the Caravan), 158–
159
HT-3 (Hallock Tailless #3):
as an indefinite idea, 76
as the Aero King or Aero Wing,
159, 160, 201
as the Pterodactyl, 201
Huáncayo, Peru, 117
Huánuco, Peru, 118
Huggins, Bill & Kitty, 215
human-factors engineering, 91, 163,
198
Hume, Tony (Naval-cadet cohort),
35–36

instrument flying:
training for, 37, 42, 69, 121
mentioned, 48, 103, 149, 159

J. C. Penney, 100
Jacobs radial engine, 88
Jamaica, 45
Johns Hopkins University, 178
Johnson, Claudia Alta (Lady Bird), 146
Johnson, Lyndon Baines (LBJ), 142–
150, 158
Jones, Al (Navy colleague), 69
Jungle Aviation and Radio Service
(JAARS), 110, 119
Junkers Ju-88, 37
Justice Department, U. S., 122

Kennedy, John F. (JFK), 143, 150
Key West, Florida, 48
Kimbro, Bill, 95
Kingston, Jamaica, 45
Kitty Hill Airfield (near Austin, Texas),
215
Kling, Rudy, 11–12
Koehler, Fred (boyhood friend), 9
Korda, Dick, 18

la mordida, 114
La Oroya, Peru, 117

Lago Vista Airport (near Austin, Texas), 217
Lake Erie, 21, 141
laminar flow, 171, 197
Langston, John, 205, 206, 208, 216
Lanzo, Chester, 18
Laredo, Texas, 125
Lauderdale, Don, 177
Lauderdale, Malcolm, 106–109
Lauson-Tecumseh engine, 154
Learjet, 168
Leyte Gulf, Battle of, 72
Lima, Peru, 110, 111, 116–117, 118, 119
Lindbergh, Charles, 5
Link trainer, 37, 40, 42
Lippisch, Alexander, 19
Lisman, Perry Hall, 177
Livermore, California, 34
lobster, importing & selling, 99–104, 111
Lockheed aircraft:
   C-56, 27
   Electra, 148–150
   Lodestar, 27, 125, 143
   P-38 Lightning, 25, 26
Los Angeles, California, 73, 190
Lost Nation Airport (Willoughby, Ohio), 21
Lycoming engines:
   IO-540-B1, 169
   GO-435, 196
   0-320, 205, 209
   mentioned, 91

Macon, USS (airship), 8
MacPherson, Eugene (father-in-law), 39, 40, 54, 83, 103, 104, 108
MacPherson, Ruth (née Hardaway) (mother-in-law), 39, 53, 83
Magdalena River, Colombia, 141
Manila, Philippines, 68, 71
Marks, Lenny, 87
Martin PBM Mariner, 44–51, 61–62
Maybach engines, 5, 7
McKain, Floyd (boyhood friend), 9
Medellín, Colombia, 141
Medina Model Makers Club, 8–10
Medina, Ohio, 1, 5, 6, 7, 8, 9, 22, 43, 63, 65, 66, 78, 79
Mexico, 83, 95, 97, 98, 99, 101, 103, 111, 114, 139, 188–189
Meyers Model 200, 160

Miami, Florida, 44, 46, 50, 51, 52, 54, 56, 59, 62, 63, 66, 119, 141
Midland, Texas, 125, 214
Miller, Jay, 216
Milwaukee, Wisconsin, 199
Minicab, 156–157
missiles, 177, 178, 179, 184–185, 190
missionaries, 109–110, 111, 117, 118–119, 123
Model Airplane News, 10
model airplanes:
   Aero King display model, 161
   Aero Wing test model, 170, 171
   Baffle Bird. (*See* Baffle Bird: large flying model)
   Bobtail. (See Bobtail)
   building and flying, 5, 8–11, 12, 14–17, 18, 23–24, 27–28, 215
   Caravan display model, 159
   Road-a-Plane display model, 93
Montgomery, Alabama, 128
Morse code, 189
Motor Rickshaw, 153–157, 181, 205, 210
Moyers, Bill, 143

N3N primary trainer, 34, 73
NASA Langley Research Center, Newport News, Virginia, 214
National Air Races, 8, 10–12, 15, 20, 91
National Transportation Safety Board (NTSB), 141
Naval Air Station Corpus Christi, 41, 42
Naval Air Station Oceana, 185
Naval Air Station Patuxent River, 73, 74
Naval Air Test Center, 74
Naval Air Transport Service (NATS), 44, 68
Naval Aircraft Factory, 73
navigation, 36, 38, 41, 49, 103
Navy Masters Field (Miami, Florida), 62
Navy, U. S.:
   advanced flight training, 42–43
   aviation cadet training, 31–36, 37–38, 40–42, 87
   mentioned, 5, 17, 38, 44, 45, 46, 57–58, 59, 60, 61, 62, 66, 68, 70, 72, 73, 74, 78, 99, 120, 121, 143, 177, 179, 181, 190

Navion, 33, 160, 194–198, 215
Netherlands Antilles, 188
Neutrality Act, 123
Newman, Jim, 86, 212, 213
Nicaragua, 112
Noorduyn Norseman (UC-64):
    description of and buying, 100–101
    federal charges involving export of, 122–124
    flying to and in Peru, 111–117, 119, 120
    hauling cargo with, 102, 103, 104
    sale of, 109–110
North American aircraft:
    AT-6, 114, 190
    B-25 Mitchell, 20, 45, 70–71, 72
    Navion, 194. *See also* Navion
    P-51 Mustang, 190, 194
Northrop aircraft:
    N1M, 23
    XB-35, 23
    YB-49, 23
Northrop, Jack, 19
Null, Luke, 208

Oak Brook Polo Grounds, Chicago, 127
Oakland, California, 33, 36, 66, 67, 68
Old Castle Inn (Miami, Florida), 54
Old-Timer competition, 17
Opa Lacka Airport (Miami, Florida), 61
Oranjestad, Aruba, 188
Orenda engine, 169
Ortman, Earl, 11–12
OX-5 engine, 2

Panagra Airways, 119
Panama, 46, 47, 49, 53, 62, 111, 112–113, 139, 141
Panama City, Panama, 113
Pan-American Highway, 139
Parker, Rocky, 84, 104
Partlon, Ronald (boyhood friend), 9
Pearl Harbor, attack on, 24
Pennsylvania Central Airlines, 43
Peru, journey to, 110, 111–120, 123, 139
Philippines, 62, 66–72, 102
Piper aircraft:
    Apache, 178
    Cherokee, 205
    Comanche, 160
    Cub, 21, 31, 32, 87, 106, 109, 200

    Tri-Pacer, 136
Poberezny, Paul, 199
Point Mugu, California, 73
polo, 127, 128
Pompano Beach, Florida, 56
Popular Aviation magazine, 8, 10
Port-au-Prince, Haiti, 45, 48
Pratt & Whitney engines:
    PT6, 169
    R-985, 41
    R-1340, 100, 114
    R-2800 Double Wasp, 70
Price, Frank, 180
profilometer, 187
propeller shroud, 161, 170–171
Pterodactyl (HT-3):
    concept and original design, 201–204
    construction, 204–209
    end of project, 209–212
    final disposition of, 218
    naming of, 202
    mentioned, 174
public aircraft status, 181, 193
Pucallpa, Peru, 118–120
Puerto Rico, 187
pusher (aircraft configuration):
    advantages of, 162–163
    propeller shroud and, 170
    mentioned, 12, 15, 23, 75, 89, 92, 158, 160, 201, 202

Quaker Oats, 8
Quillin, Monroe, 151
Quinn, Sally, 143
Quist, Charles (Charlie), 82, 86, 87, 88, 95–96
Quist, Mary, 82

radar, 59, 160, 173, 177, 178–180, 182, 184, 185, 186, 187, 188, 190–191, 192
radio control, 70, 170, 215
radome, 182–183
Ragsdale's Flying Service (Austin, Texas), 184
Rangemaster, 197–198. *See also* Navion
Rankin, Tex, 31
Recife, Brazil, 45
Redbird (LBJ's Beech Model 18), 143, 145, 147–150
Redbird Airport (Dallas, Texas), 121

Reeves, Tex, 125
rickshaw, 154. *See also* Motor Rickshaw
Rio de Janeiro, Brazil, 45
Road Wing (other names: HT-1, Baffle Bird, Road-A-Plane):
　construction, 89, 93–94, 105, 121, 122, 125, 130
　end of project, 138
　engine for, 94, 96, 105, 106
　final disposition of, 218
　flying, 130–136
　projected second prototype, 137–138
　concept and design, 75, 76, 89–93
　naming and designation of, 89, 130
　roadability of, 89–93, 105–106, 136–138
　static display model, 93
　mentioned, 126, 139, 159, 164, 199
roadability, general concept of, 89–93, 138. *See also* Road Wing: roadability of
Roanoke, Virginia, 43
Robert Mueller Municipal Airport (Austin, Texas), 85, 101, 142, 145, 148, 183, 184, 215, 216, 218
Roberts, Matt, 85
Rochester, New York, 129
Rooney Plaza Hotel (Miami, Florida), 54
Roosevelt, Franklin Delano, 25, 40, 143, 144
Rosenbaum, Henry (Navy colleague), 50
Rosy the Riveter, 29
Rutan, Burt, 201, 208
Ryan Navion, 194. *See also* Navion

Sabine River (Texas), 151
Sadler, Jerry, 151, 152
Samar, Philippines, 68, 69, 70, 72
San Antonio, Texas, 38, 97, 103, 104, 125, 126, 129, 135, 149
San Antonio Express-News, 104
San Diego, California, 186, 190
San Francisco, California, 73
San Juan, Puerto Rico, 45
San Marcos, Texas, 37
San Pedro Sula, Honduras, 112

San Salvador, El Salvador, 189
Santiago de Guayaquil, Ecuador, 116
Scripps-Howard Junior Aviator Nationals, 15–17
sea-clutter studies, 179, 186, 190
Seaplanes, 21, 44, 46, 47, 61. *See also* flying boats
Selma, Alabama, 128
Sensenich propeller, 105, 137
Serranía del Darién, 113
Servicemen's Readjustment Act of 1944. *See* GI Bill of Rights
Sikorsky XR-4, 26
Silver Springs, Maryland, 178–179
six-by-six (military truck), 71
Smith Mini-Plane, 212–213
Smithfield, Al, 18
smoke system (for aerobatics), 180–181
Society of Antique Modelers, 17
Spanish-American War, 67
sport aviation, 194, 199–204
Sport Aviation magazine, 200
St. Edward's Airport (Austin, Texas), 82–88, 97, 98, 128. *See also* Austin Aero Service
St. Edward's University (Austin, Texas), 40
St. Elmo's fire, 50–51
St. Louis, Missouri, 37, 147
St. Mary's College (Oakland, California), 33
static stress testing, 25
Stearman aircraft:
　N2S Kaydet, 34, 35, 36
　PT-17 Kaydet, 190
　mentioned, 61
Stearman, Ron, 208, 213, 214
Stetson hat, 144–145, 146, 148
Stinson aircraft:
　Detroiter (monoplane), 13
　Model 105, 21
　Model 108 Voyager, 80–81, 82, 83, 84, 85, 87, 94, 95, 96–97, 98, 99, 100, 103, 121, 134, 194
　Reliant, 94
Studebaker automobiles and engines, 12
submarines, 44, 179–180
Summer Institute of Linguistics (SIL), 110, 119, 123

TAG Airlines, 141

tailless aircraft:
    advantages of, 19, 92, 162–163
    elevator authority and, 132–133
    mentioned, 12, 15, 16, 18, 23, 24, 27, 52, 75–78, 89, 92, 120, 121, 130, 138, 158, 160, 201, 202, 215
Talara, Peru, 116
Talos guided missile, 179, 182, 185
Tampa, Florida, 98
Tampico, Mexico, 95–96, 101, 102, 125
Tapachula, Mexico, 188–189
Taylor Aerocar, 91, 92
Taylor, C. Gilbert, 18, 164
Taylor, Moult, 91, 92
Taylorcraft Corporation and aircraft, 18, 21, 79, 87, 178
Teague, Harold, 142–143, 144, 150
Teamsters Union, 129
Tegucigalpa, Honduras, 112
Texas Memorial Museum (Austin, Texas), 42
Thompson Trophy, 11
Timm N2T Tudor, 34, 35
Todd, Duane (boyhood friend), 9
Townsend, William Cameron, 109–110
Trade-a-Plane, 100, 104, 109
Trinidad, 45
Truman, Harry S., 63, 143–144
Truth or Consequences, New Mexico, 219
Turbo, Colombia, 113
Turner, Roscoe, 11
Typhon guided missile, 179, 185

Ucayali River, 118
ultralight aircraft, 202
University Airport (Austin, Texas), 101
University of Texas, 39, 53, 177, 181, 213, 214, 215, 216
Urabá, Gulf of, 113
Uvalde, Texas, 143

V5 Program, 31
VariViggen, 201
Veracruz, Mexico, 111
Vernon, Carl, 217

Virginia Beach, Virginia, 186
VJ-Day, 65
Voorhees, Koert, 166–167, 174
VR-6 Squadron, 44, 45–46, 49, 61, 62, 66
VR-7 Squadron, 62, 69
Vultee aircraft:
    BT-13 Valiant, 38, 87, 94, 121
    SNV, 37–38, 40, 87

Waco XCG-4A, 26
Waco, Texas, 180
War Bonds, 37
War Training Service (WTS), 29, 31
Waterman Arrowbile, 12, 15, 18, 89
Waterman, Waldo, 12, 15, 18, 89
Wattendorf, Frank, 22
wedding, 52–54
Weske, John R., 10, 18–19, 20, 21, 22
West Palm Beach, Florida, 56
Westland-Hill Pterodactyl, 202
White Sands Missile Range, New Mexico, 179, 180, 182, 185
Williams, Al, 17
Williams, Charles, 150
Willoughby, Ohio, 21
wind tunnel, 10, 14, 20, 22, 25, 170
Windecker Eagle, 214–215
winglets, 173
Women Airforce Service Pilots (WASP), 82
World War I (Great War), 1, 8, 19, 73
World War II:
    beginning of, 19
    end of, 63, 65, 66, 73
    effects of, 67–68, 69, 71–72, 73–74, 75
    progress of, 19, 36–37, 40, 42, 51–52, 62, 63, 67
    U. S. entry into, 24–27
Worthington Wholesale Hardware, 10
Wright Field (Dayton, Ohio), 22–27, 37, 74, 75, 89, 120
Wright R-2600-12 engine, 44
Wycliffe Bible Translators, 109–110

Yant, Charles, 196–198, 216
Yucatán Peninsula, 95, 98, 101, 111

About the Author

Austin Bruce Hallock is the eldest son of Bruce King Hallock and Enid M. Hallock. He was born in Austin, Texas, in 1947. Until recently he made his living as a technical writer. In 2008 he and his wife Leela Devi moved from Austin to Corvallis, Oregon. Although his legal given name is "Bruce Glen," he now answers to the nickname of "Austin" or "Austin Bruce." His current interests include history and fiction—both the reading and writing of them. He is an award-winning science fiction author.

The author welcomes questions and comments on this book. You may reach him at:

1975 SE Crystal Lake Dr. #222
Corvallis OR 97333
USA

phone: 541-752-1784

e-mail: AustinBruceHallock@gmail.com

www.ingramcontent.com/pod-product-compliance
Lightning Source LLC
Chambersburg PA
CBHW060509100426
42743CB00009B/1262